vegetarian dishes

vegetarian dishes

simple recipes for delicious food every day

RYLAND PETERS & SMALL

LONDON • NEW YORK

Designer Paul Tilby

Commissioning Editor Nathan Joyce

Production Controller Mai-Ling Collyer

Art Director Leslie Harrington

Editorial Director Julia Charles

Publisher Cindy Richards

Indexer Vanessa Bird

First published in 2015 by
Ryland Peters & Small
20–21 Jockey's Fields
London WC1R 4BW
and
341 East 116th Street
New York NY 10029

www.rylandpeters.com

Text © Ghillie Basan, Jordan & Jessica
Bourke, Maxine Clark, Chloe Coker &
Jane Montgomery, Amy Ruth Finegold,
Acland Geddes, Nicola Graimes, Jenny
Linford, Hannah Miles, Annie Rigg,
Laura Washburn and Ryland Peters
& Small 2015

Design and photographs © Ryland
Peters & Small 2015

ISBN: 978-1-84975-596-2

10 9 8 7 6 5 4 3 2 1

A CIP record for this book is available
from the British Library.

US Library of Congress Cataloging-in-
Publication data has been applied for.

Printed and bound in China

notes

• Both British (Metric) and American
(Imperial plus US cups) are included in
these recipes, but it is important to work
with one set of measurements and not
alternate between the two within a recipe.

• All spoon measurements are level,
unless otherwise specified.

• Ovens should be preheated to the
specified temperature. Recipes in this
book were tested using a regular oven.
If using a fan-assisted oven, follow the
manufacturer's instructions for adjusting
temperatures.

• Most cheese available to buy in
supermarkets today is suitable for
vegetarians because the traditional calf
rennet starter used to make it has been
substituted for an animal-free alternative.
However do remember that cheeses
started with animal rennet are not suitable
for strict vegetarians so read food labelling
carefully and, if necessary, check that the
cheese you buy is made with a non-animal
(microbial) starter. Traditional, handmade or
specialist cheeses found in delicatessens
are most likely to fall into this category,
but there is an increasing number of
manufacturers who are now producing
vegetarian versions of traditionally non-
vegetarian cheeses so check online for
suppliers and stockists in your location.
Traditional Parmesan is never vegetarian
so we recommend a vegetarian hard
cheese (such as Gran Moravia which has
the same texture so is ideal for grating) or
Parma (a vegan product) which adds
flavour to a finished dish.

• All eggs are medium UK/large US,
unless otherwise specified. Recipes
containing raw or partially cooked egg
should not be served to the very young,
very old, anyone with a compromised
immune system or pregnant women.

• Where a recipe calls for salt and black
pepper, use sea salt and freshly ground
black pepper if at all possible. They give
the best flavour.

contents

Enjoying a healthy vegetarian diet

There are many definitions of a vegetarian diet and many reasons why people choose to follow the diet that they do: ethical, environmental, health, religious, financial or simply personal choice. Vegetarian diets can be simply meat-free, exclude either eggs or dairy (or both), or be completely free from all animal products (vegan). It is important that when food groups are removed from a person's diet, the balance of key dietary components are considered and maintained.

what is a vegetarian diet?

There is no single definition of a vegetarian diet. Some include dairy and eggs (lacto-ovo vegetarian), whilst others may exclude dairy but eat eggs or vice versa. For the purposes of this book we have taken a broad approach to what is a vegetarian diet, including dairy and eggs. Where we have used products such as cheese and wine, vegetarian products are available. Should you follow a stricter diet, the recipes are designed to be easily adapted to suit your needs and eggs and dairy are often included as serving suggestions only.

A vegan diet does not contain any foods of animal origin such as dairy, gelatine or honey. This book contains a number of vegan recipes, which are denoted in bold in the index on pages 142–143. Many of the recipes can also be amended for a vegan diet, either by omitting ingredients or substituting with vegan alternatives such as soya/soy-based products.

Just as what it means to be vegetarian can vary widely, so can the associated nutritional needs of each vegetarian diet. While a well-balanced vegetarian diet can be a healthy choice (they are often low in saturated fat and cholesterol and naturally high in fibre/fiber and antioxidants), if not well balanced, they can be lacking in essentials such as protein, iron, omega 3, calcium and certain vitamins (in particular vitamins D and B12). This is especially true of some vegan diets. As such, extra care must be taken to make sure that an individual's diet is well balanced and nutritionally complete by ensuring that it contains a balance of food naturally rich in particular nutrients or, where necessary, including some fortified foods.

Elderly people, expectant mothers and those feeding children should take extra care to ensure that their diets are well-balanced.

Key nutrients in the vegetarian diet

carbohydrate and fibre/fiber are usually plentiful in a good vegetarian or vegan diet – eating a variety of fruit and vegetables, including skins where possible, along with bran, potatoes and wholegrains should provide everything needed.

protein is essential in any diet. Not only is it necessary to the body for growth and repair and the production of enzymes and hormones, it also makes you feel full. An average person should eat around 45–55 g/1½–2 oz. of protein a day. In a meat-free diet, it can be harder to find complete sources of protein. This can be combatted by ensuring that you eat a variety of foods during the day and by mixing different sources of protein in one dish, such as grains with pulses/legumes, nuts or seeds. Whilst soya/soy, eggs, milk and cheese are all excellent sources of protein, they can be over-used. Consider using a variety of lentils, beans, chickpeas and wholegrains in your cooking – these are often interchangeable in a recipe so just use what you have in the pantry. Quinoa is a good source of protein added to salads or used as a substitute for rice. A sprinkling of chopped nuts or seeds is a great way to add extra protein to any dish.

key vitamins and minerals can sometimes be lacking in vegetarian diets. As well as what you are eating, think about the cooking process – try to eat a substantial amount of raw vegetables or use cooking methods such as steaming and blanching to retain as much goodness as possible. As well as eating a broad range of fruit and vegetables, for those who eat dairy and/or eggs, a lot of essential vitamins (A, B2, B12 and D) can be found in milk and eggs. For those who do not eat dairy, fortified foods such as breakfast cereals and soya/soy milk are good sources of vitamins, as are green vegetables. Vitamin C, found in citrus fruit, is usually plentiful in vegetarian and vegan diets. Not only is it important for the body, it also helps to release minerals from pulses/legumes and vegetables and helps the body to absorb iron – try squeezing some lemon juice over a salad or adding it to a dressing.

calcium can easily be found in dairy produce, but those following a dairy-free diet should ensure that they include plenty of green vegetables (such as kale and broccoli), sesame seeds, beans and nuts in their diet. Calcium can also be found in soya/soy milk and fruit juices.

iron can be lacking in meat-free diets, but eating a combination of leafy green vegetables, dried fruits, beans, nuts, seeds and tofu will combat this.

fatty acids generally vegetarian diets are fairly low in saturated fat. Dairy products are a good source of fatty acids, although it is important not to be over-reliant on them. Seeds, walnuts and soya/soy are good sources of fat. Why not also try using different oils – nut oils, rapeseed and linseed oils can all be used both for cooking and flavouring.

The well-stocked vegetarian kitchen

A well-stocked store cupboard is a great starting point for creating exciting vegetarian dishes every day of the week – whether you are trying something new or need a quick solution. Here is a basic guide to the ingredients that it's a good idea to keep at home:

In the store cupboard

BAKING SUPPLIES

Flours Plain/all-purpose flour, strong bread flour, wholemeal/whole-wheat flour and chickpea/gram flour

Raising agents Fast-action yeast, baking powder and bicarbonate of/baking soda

SWEET THINGS

Sugars Brown sugar and granulated/caster sugar

Chocolate Dark/bittersweet chocolate (70 per cent cocoa)

Honey and syrups Honey, agave syrup, golden syrup/light corn syrup and maple syrup

Vanilla Good-quality vanilla extract, vanilla bean paste or dried vanilla beans

GRAINS AND PULSES/LEGUMES

Grains Rice, wild rice, barley, bulgur wheat, quinoa, couscous and rolled oats

Pulses/legumes Dried green, red and Puy/French green lentils, dried or canned kidney beans, butter/lima beans and chickpeas

DRIED FRUIT, NUTS AND SEEDS

Dried fruit Sultanas/golden raisins and apricots

Nuts Ground almonds, flaked almonds, walnut halves, hazelnuts and pine nuts

Seeds Sesame and poppy seeds

PRESERVED VEGETABLES

Tomatoes Canned chopped tomatoes and passata/strained tomatoes, sun-dried tomatoes, tomato purée/paste

Dried vegetables Porcini mushrooms

Jarred vegetables Artichokes, olives and capers

OILS AND VINEGARS

Cooking oils Olive, canola/rapeseed and vegetable

Oils for drizzling Extra virgin olive oil, sesame oil, walnut oil, hazelnut oil and truffle oil

Vinegars White, red and Sherry wine vinegars and good-quality balsamic vinegar

HERBS AND SPICES

Fresh Basil, mint, coriander/cilantro, rosemary, thyme, sage and flat-leaf parsley (ideally growing fresh in pots)

Dried herbs Oregano, rosemary and thyme

Spices Dried chilli/hot red pepper flakes, smoked paprika (pimentòn), cinnamon, turmeric, cumin and nutmeg

OTHER SEASONINGS

Good-quality stock cubes or bouillon powder

Mustards Dijon, English and wholegrain mustard

Salt and black pepper Freshly ground is always best and stock sea salt flakes as well as table salt

Spice pastes Fresh ginger, garlic, chilli/chile (minced or puréed), ready-made curry pastes (Thai and Indian), rose harissa, etc

In the fridge and freezer

DAIRY ETC.

Eggs Organic and free-range, whenever possible

Butter Both salted and unsalted for baking

Cheese Cheddar, feta and halloumi (started with non-animal rennets if preferred, see note on page 4 for further information)

Tofu Plain, marinated and smoked

FROZEN FRUIT AND VEGETABLES

Vegetables Spinach, peas, broad/fava beans and edamame (fresh soya/soy beans)

Berries 'Fruits of the forest' red berry mix, tropical fruits (mango, papaya, kiwi etc)

OTHER FROZEN FOODS

Pastry etc Frozen shortcrust, sweet shortcrust and filo/phyllo sheets, Gyoza or dumpling wrappers

Feast your eyes on a range of delightful breakfast and brunch recipes, from savoury and hearty, such as Welsh Rarebit Waffles, to sweet and fruity, like Blueberry & Coconut Muffins. There are also Multigrain Granola Bars in case you're in a rush.

breakfast & brunch

banana & almond porridge

This is a recipe for a single serving, but seeing as it involves adding one measure of oats to one and a half measures of milk, it's very easy to increase this as needed without resorting to scales or measuring jugs – simply grab a glass. The banana, almond and ground sunflower seeds enhance the flavour beautifully as well as adding nutrition.

For the stovetop method, put the oats and milk in a saucepan and bring to the boil. Lower the heat and simmer, stirring often, for 2–3 minutes. Add the banana and almonds and simmer for 1–2 minutes more, stirring often. Stir in the sunflower seeds if using.

For the microwave method, combine the oats and milk in a glass bowl and microwave on high for 1½ minutes. Remove, stir in the banana and almonds and microwave for 1 minute more. Stir in the sunflower seeds if using.

Transfer to a serving bowl, sprinkle with the cinnamon (if using), and top with a spoonful or so of honey or sugar (or one of each!). Serve immediately, with extra milk to thin and cool.

Note Ground sunflower seeds are difficult to find. However, it's possible to make them yourself by grinding the hulled seeds in a coffee grinder. The seeds are so small that this is the only machine that works. They will keep in an airtight container in the fridge for several weeks.

1 glass porridge oats

1½ glasses milk

1 small ripe banana, mashed

1–2 tablespoons ground almonds

1–2 tablespoons ground sunflower seeds (optional)

a good pinch of ground cinnamon (optional)

To serve

honey or dark, soft brown sugar

chilled milk

Serves 1

multigrain granola bars

This grab-and-go breakfast is based on English flapjacks, which usually contain only oats and lots of butter. The wheat-free mix provides a range of different grains, seeds and fruit as stealthily as possible. If you want to dress this up for a special occasion, such as a party or a cake sale, throw in some dark chocolate chips or drizzle over some melted chocolate after slicing. It's ideal for lunchboxes or after school snacks as well.

Preheat the oven to 180°C (350°F) Gas 4.

Put the butter and honey in a small saucepan and warm over low heat until just melted. Stir in the grated apple and syrup and set aside.

Combine the oats, barley flakes, millet, coconut, linseeds, almonds, raisins and salt in a large bowl and toss to combine.

Mix the melted butter mixture with the oil and stir into the dry ingredients with a wooden spoon until combined. Transfer to the prepared baking sheet and spread evenly.

Bake in the preheated oven for 10–12 minutes, until just golden around the edges for slightly chewy bars, or longer if crunchy bars are desired. Let cool slightly on the baking sheet, then cut into bars and transfer to a wire rack to cool completely. These bars will keep for 7–10 days if stored in an airtight container in the fridge.

Variation For Nutty Granola Bars, add 4–5 tablespoons nut butter, such as hazelnut or peanut (chunky or smooth) to the butter mixture.

125 g/1 stick butter

2 tablespoons honey

1 apple, unpeeled (if organic) and grated

1 generous tablespoon golden/light corn syrup

150 g/1½ cups porridge/ old-fashioned oats

100 g/1 cup barley flakes

50 g/½ cup millet or quinoa flakes

50 g/ cup desiccated coconut (unsweetened)

4 tablespoons linseeds

3 tablespoons ground almonds or sunflower seeds (optional)

a large handful of raisins

a pinch of fine sea salt

100 ml/⅓ cup rapeseed oil

a 20 x 30-cm/8 x 12-inch non-stick baking sheet, lightly greased

Makes 12–15

oatmeal pancakes with berry compote

These are fantastic breakfast pancakes – with oatmeal soaked in milk mixed into the batter and candied oats on top. Served with a warm berry compote and crème fraîche, they are the perfect pancakes to make in the summer, when you have a glut of fresh berries to use up.

Begin by preparing the compote. Put the summer berries in a saucepan or pot set over a medium heat with the water, sugar, vanilla extract/vanilla bean paste and lemon juice. Simmer until the sugar has dissolved and the fruit is just starting to soften but still holds its shape. This will take about 5 minutes. Set aside to cool then store in the refrigerator until you are ready to serve.

For the toasted oats, place the oats and sugar in a dry frying pan/skillet set over a medium heat and toast for a few minutes until the sugar starts to caramelize the oats. Remove from the heat and set aside to cool.

Soak half of the toasted oats in 250 ml/1 cup of the milk for about 30 minutes, until plump. Reserving the rest of the oats for the pancake batter.

To make the pancake batter, put the flour, baking powder, egg, salt, caster/granulated sugar and milk-soaked oats in a large mixing bowl and whisk together. Add in the melted butter and whisk again. Gradually add the remaining milk until you have a smooth, pourable batter. Be careful not to make the batter too thin when adding the remaining milk – you may not need it all. Cover and put in the refrigerator to rest for 30 minutes.

When you are ready to serve, remove your batter mixture from the refrigerator and stir once. Put a little butter in a large frying pan/skillet or a griddle pan set over a medium heat. Allow the butter to melt and coat the base of the pan, then ladle small amounts of the batter into the pan. Sprinkle some of the reserved toasted oats over the top of the pancake and cook until the underside is golden brown and a few bubbles start to appear on the top – this will take about 2–3 minutes. Turn the pancake over using a spatula and cook on the other side until golden brown. Keep the pancakes warm while you cook the remaining batter in the same way, adding a little more butter to the pan each time if required.

Serve the pancakes with the cooled berry compote and crème fraîche.

370–400 ml/1½ cups milk

200 g/1½ cups self-raising/rising flour, sifted

2 teaspoons baking powder

1 egg

a pinch of salt

1 tablespoon caster/granulated sugar

3 tablespoons melted butter, plus extra for frying

crème fraîche, to serve (optional)

For the compote

500 g/4 cups summer berries (raspberries, blueberries, strawberries and blackberries in any combination of your choosing), stalks removed

250 ml/1 cup water

100 g/½ cup caster/granulated sugar

1 teaspoon vanilla extract/vanilla bean paste

freshly squeezed juice of 1 lemon

For the toasted oats

60 g/½ cup oatmeal

50 g/¼ tablespoon caster/granulated sugar

Makes 10

blueberry & coconut muffins

500g/4 cups plain/all-purpose flour

2 teaspoons baking powder

200 g/1¾ sticks butter, softened

200 g/1 cup caster/superfine sugar

2 eggs

500 ml/2 cups whole milk

250 g/2 cups blueberries

40 g/½ cup sweetened desiccated coconut

a 12-hole muffin pan
a piping/pastry bag (optional)

Makes 12

The good old muffin: one of the most ubiquitous, well-loved breakfast treats. The base recipe remains the same, regardless of flavourings. In effect, you make your muffin mix, then add whatever you want. In this recipe it's blueberries and coconut, but pretty much anything sweet goes. Raspberries, chocolate chips, banana and cinnamon... have some fun!

Preheat the oven to 180°C (350°F) Gas 4.

Prepare your muffin pan by cutting 15-cm/6-inch squares of greaseproof/ parchment paper. Find a circular object that fits snugly into each hole of the pan, and use it to push the centre of each paper square into each section so it forms a little cup.

Sift together the flour and baking powder to remove any lumps, then set aside.

Put the butter and sugar in a large mixing bowl and beat until pale and fluffy. Add the eggs one at a time while mixing, making sure the first has been totally incorporated before adding the next. Add the milk and mix well.

Fold in the flour and baking powder until you have a thick, viscous mixture, then add the flavouring ingredients, in this case the blueberries and coconut, stirring gently so you don't crush the berries into the mixture (unless you want to, of course: it's your muffin, you can do as you please). Reserve a little coconut for sprinkling on top.

Spoon the mixture into a piping/pastry bag and pipe it into each hole, filling it about halfway up (they will grow enormously in the oven), or use a spoon.

Bake for 20 minutes, then remove and sprinkle with the remaining coconut.

pain perdu with summer berries

Pain perdu, which translates as 'lost bread' and is more commonly known as 'eggy bread', is so easy to make, and served with fresh berries and a summer berry sauce it is a very elegant breakfast.

Begin by making the sauce. Put the strawberries and raspberries in a saucepan or pot with the water and sugar set over a medium heat. Simmer for 5 minutes until the fruit is very soft. Pass through a sieve/strainer over a bowl to remove the seeds and discard them. Set aside to cool.

For the pain perdu, whisk together the eggs, cream and sugar in a mixing bowl, transfer to a shallow dish and set aside. Melt the butter in a large frying pan/skillet set over a medium heat until the butter begins to foam. Use the cutter to cut out circles from the brioche. Soak each circle in the egg mixture on one side for a few seconds, then turn over and soak the other side. The bread should be fully coated in egg, but not too soggy – it is best to soak one slice at a time. Put each circle straight into the pan before soaking the next slice.

Cook for 2–3 minutes on each side until the brioche is golden brown. Keep the cooked brioche warm while you cook the remaining slices in the same way, adding a little butter to the pan each time, if required.

Serve the toasts warm, drizzled with the berry sauce, a few fresh berries and a generous spoonful of crème fraîche. Dust with icing/confectioners' sugar and enjoy!

2 eggs

60 ml/¼ cup double/heavy cream

1 tablespoon caster/granulated sugar

1–2 tablespoons butter, for frying

6 slices brioche or white bread

For the sauce

200 g/2 cups strawberries

150 g/1 cup raspberries

150 ml/⅔ cup water

60 g/1⅓ cup caster/granulated sugar

To serve

150 g/1 cup raspberries, to serve

200 g/2 cups strawberries, to serve

crème fraîche, to serve

icing/confectioners' sugar, for dusting

9-cm/3½-inch circular cookie cutter

Serves 6

welsh rarebit waffles

200 g/1⅔ cups self-raising/rising flour, sifted

3 eggs, separated

250 ml/1 cup milk

70 g/5 tablespoons butter, melted

sea salt and freshly ground black pepper, to taste

For the roasted tomatoes

300 g/1⅔ cups vine cherry tomatoes

1–2 tablespoons olive oil

1 tablespoon balsamic glaze

1 tablespoon caster/granulated sugar

For the topping

300 g/3½ cups Cheddar cheese, grated

1 egg

2 teaspoons wholegrain mustard

1 tablespoon Worcestershire sauce, plus extra to splash

an electric or stove-top waffle iron

Serves 6

Welsh rarebit is so simple to prepare and makes a lovely brunch, whether topping toast, a crumpet or, as in this recipe, a savoury waffle. Melted cheese with mustard and tangy Worcestershire sauce served with roasted vine tomatoes and a crisp green salad – what could be better?

Preheat the oven to 180°C (350°F) Gas 4. Put the tomatoes in the roasting pan and drizzle with olive oil, the balsamic glaze and caster/granulated sugar. Season with salt and pepper and roast in the preheated oven for 20–30 minutes until the tomatoes are soft and their juices start to run. Keep warm until you are ready to serve.

To make the waffle batter, put the flour, egg yolks, milk and melted butter into a large mixing bowl. Whisk until you have a smooth batter. Season with salt and pepper. In a separate mixing bowl, whisk the egg whites to stiff peaks and then gently fold into the batter a third at a time.

Preheat the waffle iron and grease with a little butter.

Ladle some of the batter into the preheated waffle iron and cook for 2–3 minutes until golden brown. Keep warm while you cook the remaining batter and are ready to serve.

For the topping, put all the ingredients into a bowl and mix.

Spread a large spoonful of the cheese mixture over each waffle and place under a hot grill/broiler for a few minutes until the cheese melts and starts to turn golden brown. Watch carefully to make sure that the rarebit topping and waffle do not burn, turning the grill/broiler heat down if required. Splash the tops of the waffles with a few drops of Worcestershire sauce and serve immediately with the roasted tomatoes on the side.

Whether you're entertaining friends or whether you're after a late night snack, you'll find something to suit the occasion, with Breadcrumbed Halloumi Goujons and Vegetable Tempura with Wasabi Dipping Sauce just some of the tempting recipes on offer.

snacks & small bites

1 large aubergine/eggplant

2 red onions, quartered

4 garlic cloves, left whole

grated zest and freshly squeezed juice of
1 lemon

a pinch of sugar

4 tablespoons/¼ cup olive oil

For the paprika pitta crisps (optional)

5 pitta breads, halved lengthways and cut
into strips

1 tablespoon paprika (plain or smoked)

2 tablespoons olive oil

To serve

2 tablespoons pomegranate seeds (optional)

1 tablespoon extra virgin olive oil, for drizzling

salt and freshly ground black pepper

Serves 4–6

roasted aubergine & red onion dip with paprika pitta crisps

This rich and earthy dip is very similar to the popular Middle Eastern dish *baba ganoush*. It can be made the day before, and is easily adapted to include other spices such as cumin, fennel or chilli. You can also bake the pittas in cayenne pepper, sumac or five-spice powder for a slightly different flavour.

To make the roasted aubergine/eggplant and red onion dip, preheat the oven to 190°C (375°F) Gas 5.

Put the aubergine/eggplant, onions and garlic on a baking sheet and put them in the preheated oven. Bake for 40–45 minutes until soft, but remove the garlic after 10–15 minutes and the onions after 20–25 minutes.

When cooked, cut the aubergine/eggplant in half, scoop out the flesh, and put it in a blender. Squeeze the garlic cloves out of their skins, remove and discard the soft cores and skins of the onions.

Blend the aubergine/eggplant, onions, garlic, lemon zest, sugar, olive oil, and salt and pepper to a purée. Taste and adjust the seasoning with lemon juice, sugar, salt and pepper, if needed.

To make the paprika pitta crisps, turn the oven up to 200°C (400°F) Gas 6. Drizzle a fresh baking sheet with the olive oil and then sprinkle with the paprika, salt and pepper. Put the pitta bread strips on the baking sheet and mix to coat. Bake in the oven for 8 minutes until slightly coloured and crisp.

Put the dip in a serving bowl and sprinkle with pomegranate seeds, if using. Drizzle with extra virgin olive oil and serve with the pitta crisps on the side (if desired) for dipping.

white bean & spinach dip with wholegrain crostini

Using seed oils in dips is a great way to load up on your omega 3s while whipping up an elegant side dish. This is a beautiful, light, green dip that looks great garnished with fresh herbs. Serve with carrot sticks, crispy crostini, as here.

For the crostini, preheat the oven to 180°C (350°F) Gas 4.

Slice the baguette or rolls into 1-cm/½-inch slices. Brush both sides of the sliced baguette or rolls with garlic-infused olive oil then arrange the pieces on a baking sheet. Season with salt and pepper.

Bake the slices in the preheated oven for 20 minutes, turning once so both sides cook evenly and brown. Transfer the crostini to a wire rack to cool then serve with the white bean dip.

For the dip, blend all of the ingredients together in a food processor. Add the coarsely chopped spinach at the end, mix together and serve.

410 g/2½ cups white beans

freshly squeezed juice of 1 lemon

freshly squeezed juice of 1 clementine

1 peeled garlic clove

50 g/1 cup spinach

3 tablespoons flaxseed oil

Himalayan salt and freshly ground black pepper, to taste

For the crostini

1 wholegrain baguette or 6 wholegrain gluten-free rolls

120 ml/½ cup garlic-infused olive oil

Serves 4

cannellini & artichoke dip
with olive & fennel-seed grissini

Like focaccia, grissini are a cinch to make. They can be baked in advance and reheated to crisp up just before serving. This recipe may make more grissini than you need but you'll find yourself nibbling on them as soon as they come out of the oven.

To make the grissini, mix together the flour, yeast, salt and fennel seeds in a large bowl. Warm the milk in a small saucepan until it is hand-hot but not boiling, stir in the olive oil, then pour into the large bowl with the dry ingredients. Mix until the dough comes together. Lightly dust the work surface with flour, tip the dough out of the bowl and knead for about 5 minutes, or until smooth and elastic. Add the chopped olives, rosemary and cheese and knead again until thoroughly incorporated.

Shape the dough into a neat, smooth ball, return to the bowl and cover with clingfilm/plastic wrap. Leave in a warm place for about 1 hour, or until doubled in size.

Lightly dust the work surface with flour again, tip the dough out and knead for about 1 minute. Roll the dough into a rectangle roughly 5–7-mm/¼-inch thick. Cut the dough into finger-width strips, roll each strip slightly to round off the edges and arrange on 2–3 baking sheets. Let rise for 15 minutes while you preheat the oven to 180°C (350°F) Gas 4.

Bake the grissini on the middle shelf of the preheated oven for about 10 minutes, or until golden and crisp.

To make the dip, put all the ingredients in the bowl of a food processor and blend until just smooth.

Serve the warm grissini immediately with the dip.

For the grissini

375 g/3 cups (strong) white bread flour

7-g sachet/package or 3 level teaspoons fast-action/instant dried yeast

1 teaspoon fine sea salt

1 teaspoon fennel seeds, lightly crushed

225 ml/1 scant cup milk

3 tablespoons olive oil

2 tablespoons chopped green olives

2–3 teaspoons finely chopped fresh rosemary

3 tablespoons finely grated Parmesan or vegetarian alternative (see page 4)

For the cannellini & artichoke dip

400-g/14-oz. can cannellini beans, drained and rinsed

4 artichoke hearts marinated in olive oil, roughly chopped, plus 2 tablespoons oil from the jar

2 tablespoons freshly chopped flat-leaf parsley

1 large garlic clove

grated zest and freshly squeezed juice of ½ lemon

sea salt and freshly ground black pepper

Serves 4–6

30 g/2 tablespoons butter or olive oil

1 onion, grated or finely chopped

150 g/2½ cups finely chopped chestnut mushrooms

15 g/½ oz. dried porcini mushrooms, soaked in hot water until soft, and then finely chopped, reserving the soaking liquid

1 garlic clove, crushed

grated zest of 1 lemon and freshly squeezed juice of ½ a lemon

100 g/½ cup risotto rice

150 ml/⅔ cup dry white wine (optional)

300 ml/1¼ cups of vegetable stock

a small bunch of fresh parsley

50 g/⅔ cup grated Parmesan or vegetarian alternative (see page 4)

5-mm/¼-inch cubes red (bell) pepper (you could also use a few peas or diced courgette/zucchini per ball)

500 ml/about 2 cups vegetable oil, for frying

salt and freshly ground black pepper

fresh mayonnaise, to serve (optional)

For the breadcrumb coating

50 g/1⅓ cup plus 1 tablespoon plain/all-purpose flour, seasoned with salt and pepper

1 egg, lightly beaten

100 g/1¼ cups dried white breadcrumbs

Makes 16 small, or 8 large

lemon & mushroom risotto balls

Arancini (Sicilian stuffed rice balls) are a great way to serve risotto. They make a satisfying bite-sized nibble, or two larger ones can be served as a starter.

To make the risotto, melt the butter in a heavy-based saucepan set over low heat. Add the onion and cook gently for about 10 minutes, then add the mushrooms and cook until softened. Add the garlic and cook for another minute.

Turn up the heat to medium and add the lemon zest and rice. Stir well and until the rice becomes opaque. Add the white wine, if using, and stir until all the liquid has been absorbed. Add about 200 ml/¾ cup of the stock and stir until the liquid is absorbed. Add the soaking liquid from the porcini mushrooms, being careful not to add any sediment. Stir well until the liquid has been absorbed, then keep adding stock and stirring until the risotto rice is cooked (about 20 minutes) – the rice will have softened but still have a slight bite. Make sure the liquid is well evaporated – the consistency should be

thicker than a normal risotto so that the risotto balls will hold their shape. Remember that the rice mixture will thicken slightly when cooled. While the risotto is still hot, stir the cheese and parsley through it until incorporated.

Spread the rice on a large plate or tray to cool it quickly to room temperature, then form it into bite-size balls (about 40 g/1½ oz. each). To fill the balls, put each one in the palm of your hand and push down into the centre with your thumb, and put a few red pepper cubes in, then cover with the rice and roll back into a ball.

For the breadcrumb coating, place the flour, lightly beaten egg and breadcrumbs in 3 separate bowls. Roll each ball in the flour and tap off any excess. Then roll in egg and then in the breadcrumbs. For an extra crunchy coating, repeat the breadcrumb coating. Set the balls aside in the fridge until ready to fry.

Pour the vegetable oil into a deep stainless steel pan, filling it no more than halfway. Heat the oil carefully and do not allow it to smoke. It is ready when a small piece of bread takes 15–20 seconds to brown. If the oil is too hot, the outer crumb coating might burn before the centre is cooked. Cook no more than 4 balls at a time until golden brown (1–2 minutes). Drain excess oil on paper towels, and serve warm with mayonnaise, if desired.

1 tablespoon sesame oil

120 g/4 oz. shiitake mushrooms

1 pak choi/bok choy

1 carrot, grated

6 spring onions/scallions, finely sliced

2 garlic cloves

1–2 fresh red chillies/chiles

2-cm/¾-inch piece of fresh ginger, grated

a handful of fresh coriander/cilantro

1 pack of frozen round dumpling (gyoza) wrappers or wonton wrappers, defrosted

cornflour/cornstarch, for dusting

sesame oil, for frying (optional)

For the dipping sauce

3 tablespoons dark soy sauce or tamari

2 teaspoons dark brown sugar

1 tablespoon sesame oil

2 tablespoons rice vinegar (or white wine vinegar if you don't have it)

1 garlic clove, crushed

1 teaspoon finely grated fresh ginger

½–1 fresh red chilli/chile, very finely chopped

a squeeze of fresh lemon juice

a handful of fresh coriander/cilantro, chopped

a bamboo – or other – steamer, lined with parchment paper

Makes 18

vegetable dumplings with dipping sauce

These dumplings make a good sharing plate or appetizer – they can be made ahead of time and frozen. Buy the wrappers from your local Asian store or order them online and use whatever you have in the fridge for the filling. Pour the dipping sauce over some grated carrot for a quick salad or salsa.

To make the dipping sauce, put all of the ingredients in a small bowl and stir until well combined.

To make the dumplings, heat the sesame oil in a frying pan/skillet set over medium–high heat and add the mushrooms, pak choi/bok choy and carrot. Cook for about 5 minutes, until softened. Put the cooked mushrooms, pak choi/bok choy and carrots in a food processor along with the spring onions/scallions, garlic, chilli, ginger and coriander/cilantro and blitz. Alternatively, finely chop all of the ingredients by hand.

Dust the work surface with a little cornflour/cornstarch and put the dumpling wrappers on the floured surface. Put 1 teaspoon of the filling in the centre of each wrapper. Using a pastry brush, moisten the edges of each wrapper with a little water, then seal the edges together. Make sure that the dumpling is well sealed – if not, add a little more water to seal it. You can use your finger to frill the edge of the dumpling for decoration.

Put the bamboo steamer over a pan of boiling water. If you do not have a steamer, cover a colander with a make-shift parchment paper lid. Put the dumplings in the parchment-lined steamer, cover with a lid and steam for 10–15 minutes until the filling is hot and cooked.

For extra flavour and texture, once the dumplings have been steamed, heat a tablespoon of sesame oil in a frying pan/skillet over a high heat and fry the dumplings for 1–2 minutes, until the bottom and sides start to colour. Be careful as they colour quickly and can easily burn.

The uncooked dumplings will keep covered in the fridge for a few hours. Alternatively, steam the dumplings, let them cool, then store them, well wrapped, in the fridge for a few hours. Resteam until they are hot again.

chicory leaves stuffed with beetroot, cumin & mixed grains

This tasty and colourful salad makes a great addition to any buffet. The chicory leaf gives a bitter edge to cut through the sweetness of the beetroot. It's a good dish to prepare in advance, but hold back some herbs and pistachios to sprinkle on top, as the beetroot colours everything.

Wash the rice well and put it in a large saucepan with boiling salted water and the cardamon pods. Cook according to the packet instructions until soft but still with a bite. Strain well, spread on a tray to cool down and set aside.

Meanwhile, cook the quinoa in boiling salted water – just enough to cover the grains by 5 mm/¼ inch. Gently simmer for about 10 minutes, until softened but retaining a bite. Strain well, spread on a tray to cool down and set aside.

Lightly toast the cumin and fennel seeds in a dry frying pan/skillet set over a medium heat – just until you can smell the aromas of the seeds releasing – then turn off the heat, remove from the pan and set aside.

In a bowl, combine the chickpeas, rice, quinoa, lime zest, coriander/cilantro, cumin seeds and fennel seeds, beetroot/beet, pistachios, salt and pepper, and mix well.

Taste the mixture and season with the oil, lime juice, sugar, salt and pepper. Once seasoned, fill the chicory/Belgian endive leaves generously and sprinkle with coriander/cilantro and the remaining pistachios.

* Note: if using dried chickpeas, these will need to be soaked overnight and cooked in simmering water for about 15 minutes before use.

50 g/generous ¼ cup basmati rice

5 cardamon pods

50 g/heaped ¼ cup quinoa

2 teaspoons cumin seeds

2 teaspoons fennel seeds

100 g/¾ cup canned chickpeas*, strained and rinsed well

grated zest and freshly squeezed juice of 2 limes

a small handful of fresh coriander/cilantro leaves, finely chopped, plus extra to serve

½ raw beetroot/beet, peeled and grated (gloves are advisable as beetroot dyes your hands)

70 g/½ cup pistachios, whole or roughly chopped, plus extra

To serve

2 tablespoons groundnut/peanut oil (or olive oil, rapeseed/canola oil all work well)

a pinch of sugar

15 middle-outer chicory/Belgian endive leaves, washed and dried

salt and freshly ground black pepper

Makes 15

1 large courgette/zucchini, core removed and discarded, flesh cut into 1 x 5-cm/⅜ x 2-inch strips

1 large aubergine/eggplant, cut into rings

500 ml/about 2 cups vegetable oil, for frying

40 g/⅓ cup plain/all-purpose flour

60 g/½ cup plus 1½ tablespoons cornflour/cornstarch

¼ teaspoon baking powder

100–150 ml/⅓–⅔ cup iced sparkling/soda water

a pinch of salt

½ head of cauliflower, cut into bite-size florets

½ head of broccoli, cut into bite-size florets

3 red (bell) peppers, deseeded and cut into strips

For the wasabi dipping sauce

2 teaspoons wasabi powder

2 tablespoons sesame oil

1 tablespoon Thai fish sauce

zest and freshly squeezed juice of 1 lime

1 fresh red chilli/chile, finely chopped

2 tablespoons soy sauce

3-cm/1¼-inch piece of fresh ginger, peeled and grated

a pinch of sugar or 1 teaspoon maple syrup

Makes 4–6 servings

vegetable tempura with wasabi dipping sauce

This is a take on a Japanese classic, which is quick and simple. Great as a nibble or appetizer, serve with a dipping sauce, soy sauce, sweet chilli sauce or simply a squeeze of lemon juice. Tempura gives the traditional crudités a modern twist, and a more interesting texture for just a little extra effort.

For best results, place the courgette/zucchini and aubergine/eggplant in a sieve/strainer and sprinkle all over with table salt, then leave for 10 minutes; you will notice liquid has leached out of the vegetables. Rinse well in water to remove the salt and pat dry.

To make the wasabi dipping sauce, put the wasabi powder in a bowl and gradually add the sesame oil to form a smooth paste. Slowly add the fish sauce, lime zest and juice, and the chilli/chile, soy sauce, ginger and sugar, while continually stirring to thoroughly combine. Taste, and alter seasoning if necessary.

Set your deep-fat fryer to 190°C (375°F), or fill a wide deep saucepan ⅓ full with vegetable oil and set over a medium heat.

Make the batter immediately before cooking. Combine the flour, cornflour/cornstarch and baking powder in a bowl. Add the water to the flour mixture, whisking to combine quickly, but stop as soon as the liquid is combined — the odd lump is ok, and better than over-working the batter. The consistency should be slightly looser than a crêpe batter — a light coating batter is what you want, not one that is thick and gloopy. The batter also must be ice cold, so drop an ice cube in the batter to keep it chilled while using.

As soon as the oil has come to temperature (it's ready when a small piece of bread dropped into the pan turns golden-brown in 10–15 seconds), make sure the vegetables are dry and then dip them in the batter, shake off any excess and put them into the hot oil using a slotted metal spoon. Cook for 1–2 minutes until pale golden (tempura does not colour like other batter so do not wait for a deep colour). Repeat, cooking in small batches as cooking too much at the same time can reduce the oil temperature. When cooked, put the tempura on paper towels to drain and lightly sprinkle with salt. Serve immediately with wasabi dipping sauce or a squeeze of lemon.

cream cheese & olive parcels

These delicious, Mediterranean-flavoured nibbles are perfect appetizers to serve with drinks.

Preheat the oven to 200°C (400°F) Gas 6.

Heat the olive oil in a small frying pan/skillet and fry the spring onions/scallions until softened. Set aside until cool.

In a mixing bowl, mix the cream cheese, fried spring onions/scallions, olives and dill. Season with a generous grinding of black pepper.

Slice the filo/phyllo sheets in half lengthways, forming 12 rectangular strips.

Brush one of the strips with melted butter (keeping the remaining sheets covered with clingfilm/plastic wrap to prevent them drying out). Place a generous teaspoon of the cream cheese mixture on the buttered filo/phyllo strip 2 cm/ 1 inch from the bottom. Take the bottom left corner of the strip and fold it up and over the filling, to form a triangular shape. then across again to the other side. Continue until you have formed a tightly closed triangular parcel. Brush on a little extra melted butter to seal the last flap into place and then place on a greased baking sheet. Brush the parcel generously with melted butter and sprinkle over a few sesame seeds.

Repeat the process with the remaining filo/phyllo strips, making 12 parcels in total.

Bake them in the preheated oven for 15–20 minutes until golden-brown. Serve warm or at room temperature.

1 teaspoon olive oil

3 spring onions/scallions, finely chopped

200 g/1 cup cream cheese

40 g/⅓ cup stoned/pitted green olives, chopped

1 tablespoon finely chopped fresh dill

freshly ground black pepper

6 rectangular filo/phyllo sheets

50 g/3½ tablespoons unsalted butter, melted

sesame seeds, for garnish

Makes 12

breadcrumbed halloumi goujons

Served warm and oozing with melted halloumi cheese, these breadcrumbed bites are really hard to resist! To add a little heat, try adding a pinch of hot smoked paprika to the breadcrumbs.

For the breadcrumb coating, put the flour, egg and breadcrumbs in 3 separate bowls. Take the slices of halloumi and coat them in flour, tapping off any excess. Next, coat them in the egg and, finally, coat them in the breadcrumbs. For an extra crunchy coating repeat the process.

If you have a deep-fat fryer, set the temperature to 160°C (325°F); if not, pour the vegetable oil into a deep stainless steel pan and fill no more than half-full with oil. To test the temperature of the oil, place a small piece of bread in the pan — it should take 10–15 seconds to turn golden brown.

Put the breadcrumbed halloumi into the hot oil and fry until golden brown (this will take 3–4 minutes). Dry off the halloumi on paper towels and sprinkle with sea salt. Serve warm with lemon wedges for squeezing.

50 g/⅓ cup plus 1 tablespoon plain/all-purpose flour, seasoned with salt and pepper

1 egg, lightly beaten

150 g/2 cups dried white breadcrumbs

a pinch of smoked hot paprika (optional)

250 g/9 oz. halloumi, cut into 8 slices

500 ml/about 2 cups vegetable oil, for frying

salt and freshly ground black pepper

lemon wedges, to serve

Makes 8

For the falafel

225 g/1 cup dried chickpeas

1 small red onion

3 garlic cloves

2 tablespoons ground coriander

2 tablespoons ground cumin

1 large bunch fresh coriander/cilantro

1 large bunch fresh flat-leaf parsley

2 slices rustic white bread, crusts removed

4 tablespoons olive oil

vegetable oil, for frying

sea salt and freshly ground black pepper

For the tzatziki

1 cucumber

350 g/1½ cups thick Greek yogurt

freshly squeezed juice of ½ lemon

1 small bunch fresh mint, chopped

1 garlic clove, crushed

sea salt

a deep-fat fryer (optional)

Makes 20–30

falafel with tzatziki

The secret to this delicious snack is the large amount of fresh coriander/cilantro and flat leaf parsley, which not only give the mixture fragrance and a brilliantly vibrant green colour, but also help keep it moist. They're best eaten as soon as they're fried and still gently warm on the inside. Leave them out too long, and the lovely crunchy exterior will go soft and spongy.

Give the chickpeas a quick rinse, then leave them to soak in plenty of water overnight.

Once soaked, put the chickpeas, along with all the other falafel ingredients except the vegetable oil, in a food processor and blend to a rough paste. Avoid the temptation of blending it too much; the falafel should still have texture when you bite into it.

Heat the vegetable oil to 180°C (350°F) in a deep-fat fryer or fill a wide deep saucepan ⅓ full with vegetable oil and set over a medium heat. Take a scoop of the mixture and mould it into a rough ball shape with your hands. As soon as the oil has come to temperature (it's ready when a small piece of bread dropped into the pan turns golden-brown in 10–15 seconds), fry the falafels in batches until they are very dark brown (they will colour quickly, but avoid the temptation to remove them from the oil. They need to fry for at least 3–4 minutes in order to crisp up properly). Remove and allow to cool on a wire rack.

For the tzatziki, cut the cucumber in half lengthwise. Use a teaspoon to scoop out the seeds and discard them. Grate the rest of the cucumber, then mix it with a little salt and leave in a colander to drain for 10 minutes (this helps remove the excess liquid, which would otherwise dilute your tzatziki). Stir the yogurt, lemon juice, mint and garlic into the cucumber. Season with extra salt if necessary, and serve with the falafel.

sweet potato, spinach & goat's cheese quesadilla

In this delicious recipe, the sweetness of the potatoes is perfectly complemented by the salty tang of the cheese and the smoky flavour of the chipotle chillies/chiles.

Preheat the oven to 120°C (250°F) Gas ½.

Boil, steam or roast the sweet potatoes until tender and leave to cool. When cool, mash the flesh with the chilli/chile and salt. Taste and adjust the seasoning and set aside. Put the spinach in a large saucepan, cover and set over low heat just to wilt. Allow to cool, then squeeze out any excess moisture from the cooked spinach using your hands. Chop finely and set aside until needed.

To assemble the quesadillas, spread 2–3 tablespoons of sweet potato purée on 4 of the tortillas. Dot the spinach evenly over the surface and add a quarter of the cheese slices. Top with another tortilla.

Heat the remaining oil in a non-stick frying pan/skillet set over medium heat. When hot, add a quesadilla, lower the heat and cook for 2–3 minutes until golden on one side and the cheese begins to melt. Turn over and cook the other side for 2–3 minutes. Transfer to a heatproof plate and keep warm in the preheated oven while you cook the rest.

To serve, top each quesadilla with sour cream. Cut into wedges, top with sprigs of coriander/cilantro and serve immediately with lemon wedges for squeezing.

800 g/1 lb. 12 oz. sweet potatoes, cut into chunks

1 large chipotle chilli/chile in adobo sauce, finely chopped plus 1 teaspoon of adobo sauce

1 teaspoon fine sea salt

200 g/3½ cups fresh spinach

8 large flour tortillas

150-g/5½-oz. log of goat's cheese, thinly sliced

vegetable oil

To serve

sour cream

sprigs of fresh coriander/cilantro

lemon wedges

Serves 4–6

Choose from refreshing summer soups to hearty winter warmers, while salads include vibrant Pearl Barley, Roast Pumpkin & Green Bean Salad and a tangy Avocado, Rocket & Grapefruit Salad with Sunflower Seeds.

soups & salads

roasted tomato & red pepper soup with cheese scones

With its rich colour and depth of flavour, this simple soup is guaranteed to please every time. It can be served hot or cold depending on the season.

Preheat the oven to 200°C (400°F) Gas 6.

To make the soup, put the onions, garlic, tomatoes and peppers on a greased baking sheet. Sprinkle with the olive oil and salt and pepper and bake for about 30 minutes until the onions and tomatoes are soft and the peppers slightly coloured. Check the garlic after 10–15 minutes and remove from the oven when soft.

Put the peppers in a sealed plastic bag or wrap in clingfilm/plastic wrap and let them cool. Remove the skins from the tomatoes and reserve the flesh in a bowl. Squeeze out the garlic cloves from their skins into the same bowl. Remove any crisp skin from the onions and add the flesh to the garlic and tomatoes.

When the peppers are cool enough to handle, gently remove the skin and put the flesh in the bowl with the other ingredients and add the stock, sugar, canned tomatoes, and salt and pepper to taste. Blend the mixture in a liquidizer/blender until very smooth. Taste and adjust the seasoning if needed.

To make the cheese scones, preheat the oven to 220°C (425°F) Gas 8. Sift the flour and salt together in a mixing bowl. Rub in the butter using a food processor or your finger tips until it resembles breadcrumbs, then stir in the cheese.

Make a well in the middle of the flour mixture. Add the egg and milk and combine well. Form the dough by kneading gently until just brought together and smooth. On a lightly floured surface, roll out to a thickness of 2.5 cm/1 inch before putting on a lightly floured baking sheet. Stamp out rounds with the cutter, using a downwards motion without twisting. Brush the scones with the egg and dusting with flour. Bake for 15 minutes until well risen and lightly golden.

Ladle the soup into serving bowls and scatter with chopped fresh basil. Swirl a spoonful of sour cream into each bowl, if liked, and serve hot or cold with the cheese scones on the side, if liked.

2 medium red onions, quartered

2 garlic cloves, unpeeled

5 plum tomatoes, halved

4 red (bell) peppers, halved and deseeded

2 tablespoons olive oil

300 ml/1¼ cups vegetable stock

a pinch of sugar

400-g/14-oz. can chopped tomatoes

salt and freshly ground black pepper

For the cheese scones (optional)

250 g/scant 2 cups self-raising/
rising flour, plus extra for dusting

⅓ teaspoon salt

55 g/¼ cup butter

30 g/⅓ cup grated mature/sharp Cheddar

1 egg, beaten

130 ml/⅓ cup semi-skimmed/
2 per cent milk

1 teaspoon English mustard

1 egg, lightly beaten, to glaze

To serve

1 tablespoon finely chopped fresh basil
(optional)

4–6 teaspoons of crème fraîche
or sour cream (optional)

a baking sheet, lightly floured
a fluted scone/biscuit cutter

Serves 4–6

curried lentil soup with fresh herb purée

The tasty herb purée adds a light, fresh touch to this comforting soup, making it a dish to curl up with all year round.

To make the soup, heat the vegetable oil in a saucepan set over a low heat and add the shallots. Cover and cook gently for about 5–10 minutes until the shallots have softened but have not taken on any colour. Add the garlic, chilli/chile and spices and cook for 2 minutes. Add the sweet potato and lentils and stir until well incorporated. Pour in enough stock to cover the ingredients.

Bring to the boil, then cover and simmer over a low heat for 45–60 minutes, until the lentils and potatoes are very soft.

For a smooth soup, give the mixture a good stir to break down the lentils. Season generously with salt and pepper and stir the extra virgin olive oil through the soup.

To make the herb purée, put all the ingredients in a food processor and blitz until they form a smooth paste. Ladle into serving bowls and swirl a spoonful of herb purée into each bowl. Serve hot with chunks of crusty bread.

1 tablespoon vegetable oil

2 shallots, finely chopped

4 garlic cloves, crushed

1 fresh red chilli/chile, finely chopped

2 teaspoons turmeric

½ teaspoon garam masala

1 medium sweet potato, chopped

250 g/1⅓ cups dried red split lentils, rinsed and drained

500 ml/2 cups vegetable stock

1 tablespoon extra virgin olive oil

salt and freshly ground black pepper

chunks of crusty bread, to serve (optional)

For the fresh herb purée

1 tomato

1 garlic clove

2-cm/¾-inch piece of fresh ginger, peeled

1 fresh red chilli/chile

a handful of fresh coriander/cilantro

1 tablespoon vegetable oil

Serves 4–6

chilled mint & cucumber soup with parmesan crisps

This refreshing, chilled soup is perfect for a warm summer's day. If you are not a fan of chilled soups, we urge you to give this recipe a try and be converted. It is easy to make in advance and will keep for a day in the fridge, ready to serve. The Parmesan crisps add extra texture but are optional.

6 English cucumbers, peeled, cores removed, and flesh chopped into chunks

a small handful of fresh mint, roughly chopped

460 ml/¼ cup crème fraîche or sour cream

freshly grated zest of 1 lemon and freshly squeezed lemon juice, to taste

1½ garlic cloves, crushed

1 teaspoon sugar

salt and freshly ground black pepper

For the Parmesan crisps (optional)

50 g/1¾ oz. Parmesan or vegetarian alternative (see page 4)

Serves 4–6

To make the cucumber soup, put the cucumber and mint in a food blender and blitz to a purée. Push the purée through a fine-mesh sieve/strainer using the back of a ladle – it will look quite watery.

Put half of the pulp left in the sieve/strainer back into the blender along with the watery mixture. Add the crème fraîche/sour cream, lemon zest, garlic, sugar and salt and pepper, then blitz until combined. Taste the mixture and season with lemon juice, sugar and salt and pepper. This soup needs to be highly seasoned to bring out the delicate flavours.

Preheat the oven to 180°C (350°F) Gas 4.

To make the Parmesan crisps, spread thin strips of grated Parmesan on a baking sheet lined with parchment paper. Ensure you leave a good space between each strip as they will spread in the oven.

Bake in the oven for 7 minutes until the Parmesan (or vegetarian alternative) melts and colours slightly. Remove from the oven and remove the crisps with a palette knife. Put the crisps on a cooling rack until cooled and crisp.

Ladle the soup into serving bowls and put an ice cube in each bowl of soup to keep well chilled. Top with the Parmesan crisps and serve immediately.

black bean soup with super chia garnish

There is nothing wrong with using canned beans to create a super, fresh-tasting, easy dinner. Hiding a super seed in the salsa adds an extra health punch too!

For the super chia garnish, toss all the ingredients in a bowl and chill in the refrigerator while you make the soup so the chia seeds expand.

Heat the oil in a frying pan/skillet and fry the onion, cumin seeds, coriander and chilli powders over a medium heat for 5–8 minutes until the onions are translucent. Add the garlic and fry for a minute longer. Then add the chopped tomatoes, water and black beans and stir. Reduce the temperature, cover and cook for 15 minutes. Set aside to cool.

Once cooled, purée the soup in a food processor. Adjust the seasoning if required. Return to the heat and warm through. Serve in bowls, with a squeeze of lime juice (about a teaspoon each) and garnish with fresh coriander/cilantro and a dollop of the garnish.

2 tablespoons vegetable oil

1 large onion, finely chopped

1 teaspoon cumin seeds

1 teaspoon ground coriander

1 teaspoon chilli powder

2 garlic cloves, finely chopped

200 g/7 oz canned chopped tomatoes

950 ml/4 cups water

425 g/15 oz. black beans

2 teaspoons freshly squeezed lime juice

1 tablespoon chopped coriander/cilantro

sea salt and freshly ground black pepper, to taste

For the super chia garnish

1 tablespoon chia seeds

4 tablespoons crème fraîche or sour cream

1 teaspoon freshly squeezed lime juice

a pinch of sea salt

Serves 4

cauliflower soup
with roasted pumpkin seeds

This soup tastes really creamy, but doesn't actually contain cream. The trick is to use a generous amount of cauliflower and a good quality food processor to purée it to the right consistency. Another trick is to add a little coconut milk, which can fool any dairy lover. Try and resist the urge to munch on the roasted pumpkin seeds before they make it into the soup as a garnish, though!

30 g/¼ cup pumpkin seeds

2 teaspoons Himalayan salt

1 medium onion, chopped

1 tablespoon olive oil

3 garlic cloves, chopped

1 large head cauliflower (cut into small florets)

1 tablespoon butter

480 ml/2 cups water

700 ml/3 cups vegetable stock

120 ml/½ cup unsweetened light coconut milk

Serves 4–6

Prepare the roasted pumpkin seeds in advance. Preheat the oven to 150°C (300°F) Gas 2. Spread the seeds evenly on an oiled baking sheet and sprinkle half of the salt on top. Roast for about 30 minutes, checking on them after 15 minutes to make sure they are toasting evenly.

In a large saucepan or pot, fry the onion in olive oil over a medium–high heat for about 5 minutes or until translucent. Lower the heat slightly, add the garlic, and fry for another minute or so. Remove from the heat.

In a separate frying pan/skillet, fry half of the cauliflower in the butter. Cook until the cauliflower is toasted. Transfer the cooked cauliflower into a bowl and set aside. Repeat the cooking process with the rest of the cauliflower – this prevents overcrowding in the pan/skillet to make sure all the ingredients are cooked evenly.

Once your cauliflower is cooked, add it all to the pan of fried onion and garlic with the water, remaining salt and vegetable stock. Bring to the boil, then cover and simmer for 30 minutes. Remove from the heat and stir in the coconut milk.

Purée the soup in a food processor. Return to the heat and warm through. To serve, ladle the soup into bowls and garnish with the pumpkin seeds.

lentil & squash soup

Red lentils are quick to cook, tasty, and easy to digest. Together with squash, they also marry well with spices, such as turmeric, ginger and coriander, which are great for digestive health. It's a good idea to make a big batch of this soup because it freezes really well.

In a large saucepan or pot, fry the onions and salt in vegetable oil until the onions are soft. Add the garlic, ginger and spices and fry for about 1 minute.

Put the lentils in the bottom of the pan and coat them with the spice mixture. Add the water, vegetable stock and squash and bring to the boil. Reduce the heat, cover and simmer for about 20–30 minutes. Set aside to cool slightly.

Once cooled, purée the soup in a food processor, add the flaxseed oil and adjust the seasoning as required. Return to the heat and warm through.

Serve in bowls and garnish with fresh coriander/cilantro. The soup can be stored in the freezer for up to 3 months.

1 large onion, finely chopped

2 teaspoons sea salt

2 tablespoons vegetable oil

2 garlic cloves, chopped

1 teaspoon chopped fresh ginger

2 teaspoons ground cumin

1 teaspoon chilli powder

1 teaspoon turmeric

2 teaspoons ground coriander

350 g/2 cups red lentils

1.4 litres/6 cups water

500 ml/2 cups vegetable stock

500 g/3 cups chopped butternut squash

2 tablespoons flaxseed oil

a handful of fresh coriander/cilantro, to garnish

Serves 8–10

spinach yogurt soup with caramelized butter

Using yogurt in this delicately-flavoured soup gives it a subtle tang. For a light meal, serve it with crusty bread.

Heat the olive oil in a large, heavy-based frying pan/skillet. Add the onion and fry gently, stirring often, for 5 minutes, until softened. Sprinkle in the cumin and chilli/hot red pepper flakes and mix together.

Add the stock, season with salt and pepper and bring to the boil, then reduce the heat and simmer gently for 5 minutes.

Meanwhile, caramelize the butter by gently melting it in a small saucepan until a white sediment appears. Continue cooking over a very low heat, stirring now and then, until the white sediment turns brown and the butter has a nutty fragrance.

While the butter is caramelizing, add the spinach to the simmering soup and cook gently for 2–3 minutes.

Meanwhile, whisk together the yogurt, egg and flour until well-mixed. Add the yogurt mixture to the gently simmering soup and continue cooking over a low heat for 3–4 minutes. Stir continuously and make sure that the soup does not come to the boil.

Stir in the caramelized butter, sprinkle with sumac, if desired, and serve at once.

2 tablespoons olive oil

1 onion, finely chopped

1 teaspoon ground cumin

½ teaspoon chilli/hot red pepper flakes

800 ml/3¼ cups chicken or vegetable stock

salt and freshly ground black pepper

1 bunch of spinach, chopped

175 g/scant 1 cup yogurt

1 egg

2 teaspoons plain/all-purpose flour

40 g/3 tablespoons butter

a sprinkling of ground sumac (optional)

Serves 4

broad bean, feta & dill salad

The season for fresh, young broad/fava beans is short. They need very little preparation: just throw them into some boiling water, rinse, drain and add to pastas, risottos and salads, among other dishes. Older and frozen broad/fava beans can be used but they need a little more attention as their skins are tougher.

500 g/1 lb. shelled fresh young broad/fava beans or butter beans

65 ml/¼ cup olive oil

1 small red onion, finely chopped

2 garlic cloves, finely chopped

2 tablespoons freshly squeezed lemon juice

a small bunch of fresh dill, finely chopped

a handful of fresh flat-leaf parsley leaves

a handful of small fresh mint leaves

100 g/1 cup roughly crumbled feta

freshly ground black pepper

Serves 4

Cook the broad/fava beans in a large saucepan of boiling water for 10 minutes. Rinse under cold water and drain well. (If using older broad/fava beans, slip the skins off now and discard.)

Heat 1 tablespoon of the oil in a small frying pan/skillet set over a medium heat. Add the onion and garlic and cook for 2–3 minutes, until just softened. Remove from the heat.

Put the broad/fava beans and herbs in a bowl. In a small bowl, use a fork to mix together the remaining oil and lemon juice and then pour over the salad.

Stir to combine. Add the feta, stir again, and season well with pepper before serving.

beetroot, quinoa & green bean salad with spicy ginger dressing & shallot crisps

This exotic salad uses quinoa, an excellent, gluten-free alternative to staples such as couscous. Quinoa is a great addition to a vegetarian diet as it is a complete protein source and very rich in fibre. For an extra crunchy texture, sprinkle the salad with shallot crisps – they make a great topping for soups too.

Preheat the oven to 200°C (400°F) Gas 6.

Wrap the beetroot/beets in kitchen foil and roast them in the oven for 30 minutes until they have begun to soften. Allow to cool and cut into bite-sized pieces.

Bring a saucepan of water to the boil and cook the green beans for about 4 minutes until they are just cooked but still have a bite to them. Once the beans are cooked, plunge them into a bowl of cold water to stop the cooking process.

Put the quinoa and vegetable stock in a saucepan. Bring to the boil, then simmer for about 15 minutes until the grains are cooked and the stock has been absorbed. Remove from the heat, cover the pan and let the quinoa steam for 5 minutes, then fluff up with a fork.

To make the onion crisps, toss the shallot in the gram/chickpea flour until well covered. Put 1 cm/⅜ inch of oil in a deep pan or wok and set over a medium-high heat. Do not allow the oil to become so hot that it smokes and spits. Drop the coated shallot slices into the pan and fry for 30 seconds until they are crisp and golden. Drain on paper towels and sprinkle with salt.

To make the dressing, put all of the ingredients in a bowl and whisk until well incorporated. Season with salt and pepper.

To assemble the salad, put all the ingredients into a large bowl. Toss with the dressing, then serve on plates with a sprinkling of onion crisps.

2 raw beetroot/beets, skin on

a large handful of green beans

100 g/1 cup quinoa

250 ml/1 cup vegetable stock

a handful of toasted pistachios

200 g/1½ cups canned chickpeas

2 oranges, peeled and sliced into thin rounds

For the shallot crisps

1 shallot, finely sliced

3 tablespoons seasoned gram/chickpea flour

vegetable oil, for frying

For the spicy ginger dressing

grated zest and freshly squeezed juice of ½ an orange

freshly squeezed juice of ½ a lemon

1 garlic clove, crushed

2-cm/¾-inch piece of fresh ginger, finely chopped or grated

½–1 fresh red chilli/chile, finely diced

a handful of fresh mint, finely chopped

salt and freshly ground black pepper

Serves 2–4

warm curried lentil salad with paneer or tofu & a spiced dressing

This fresh and tasty salad is mildly spiced and perfect with either fried paneer or marinated tofu, for a vegan version. The salad itself keeps well so can be made in advance, allowing the flavours to develop.

To make the spiced dressing, heat half the oil in a small saucepan. Add the shallot and cook over a low heat for 5 minutes, until it starts to soften but still has a slight bite and has not taken on any colour. Add the remaining oil, mustard seeds, garam masala, turmeric, dried chilli/hot red pepper flakes, garlic and sugar, and cook for 2 minutes. Turn off the heat and add the vinegar, sultanas/golden raisins and fresh chilli/chile.

For the salad, put the lentils, celery, carrots, toasted cashews, mango and lime zest in a large bowl. Pour in the warm dressing, reserving about 2 tablespoons to serve, and stir until well combined and coated in the dressing.

To cook the paneer or tofu, heat the oil in a frying pan/skillet and fry the slices until golden on both sides, using tongs to turn halfway through cooking.

Brush the paneer or tofu slices with the reserved dressing and serve on top of the salad. Finish the salad with fresh mint or coriander/cilantro, and with lime wedges on the side for squeezing.

400-g/14-oz. can green lentils

2 sticks celery, finely sliced

2 carrots, grated

50 g/heaped ⅓ cup cashews, toasted

½ mango, cut in half and sliced lengthways

finely grated zest of ½ a lime

1 tablespoon vegetable oil

200 g/7 oz. paneer or tofu, sliced

a handful of fresh mint or coriander/cilantro leaves, chopped

lime wedges, to serve

For the spiced dressing

4 tablespoons vegetable oil

1 shallot, finely chopped

½ teaspoon mustard seeds

1 teaspoon garam masala

½ teaspoon turmeric

a pinch of dried chilli/hot red pepper flakes

1 garlic clove, crushed

1 teaspoon sugar

1 tablespoon white wine vinegar

50 g/⅓ cup sultanas/golden raisins

½ fresh red chilli/chile, deseeded and finely diced

Serves 2–4

avocado, rocket & grapefruit salad with sunflower seeds

This is an elegant, simple and classic appetizer. Sunflower seeds and flaxseed oil boost the omega-3 content, making this dish even healthier. Use Champagne vinegar if you're lucky enough to have some, otherwise white wine vinegar will work fine.

2 medium ripe avocados

2 pink grapefruits

100 g/4 cups rocket/arugula

For the vinaigrette

1 teaspoon clear honey

3 tablespoons Champagne vinegar or white wine vinegar

4 tablespoons flaxseed oil

3 tablespoons sunflower seeds

sea salt and freshly ground black pepper, to taste

Serves 4

Prepare the avocados. Using a sharp knife, cut an avocado in half, turning it as you do to cut around the stone. Twist the two halves to separate. Remove the stone and peel the two halves. Repeat with the second avocado then slice the flesh and set aside.

Now prepare the grapefruit. Peel the fruit whole then break into individual segments. Using a sharp knife, carefully score the straight edge of each segment then peel the membrane from the flesh. Repeat until you have released all the deliciously juicy segments.

For the vinaigrette, whisk the honey, Champagne vinegar and flaxseed oil together in a mixing bowl, adding the sunflower seeds at the last minute so as not to damage them. Season to taste.

Place a layer of rocket/arugula on each plate. Arrange the grapefruit and avocado on top, with alternating slices of grapefruit and avocado in concentric semi-circles. You needn't arrange the fruit in this way if you're in a hurry but it looks great when entertaining. Lightly drizzle a line of vinaigrette horizontally across the half-moons of alternating grapefruit and avocado. Enjoy immediately.

shredded carrot & courgette salad

Vegetables take on a completely new personality when they are prepared differently. Japanese cuisine can transform a simple radish into a piece of art. The simple act of shredding vegetables and mixing in a delicious dressing is a tasty and beautiful way to eat.

Put the carrots, courgettes/zucchini, sesame seeds and tofu in a bowl. The tofu is optional but it goes so well with the miso dressing and it transforms this dish from a side to a main meal.

For the dressing, whisk all of the ingredients together to an emulsion. Pour over the mixed salad and serve.

The salad can be prepared in advance and stored in the refrigerator for up to 2 days.

2 carrots, grated

3 courgettes/zucchini, grated

30 g/¼ cup sesame seeds

150 g/1 cup firm tofu, chopped (optional)

For the miso dressing

2 tablespoons miso paste

1 tablespoon rice wine vinegar

1 tablespoon sesame oil

2 tablespoons flaxseed oil

1 teaspoon finely sliced fresh ginger

2 teaspoons clear honey

Serves 2–4

wheatberry salad with apples & pecans

This variant of the American classic Waldorf salad uses pecans instead of walnuts and features wheatberries, which hold it together nicely and give it a lovely depth.

Put the wheatberries in a medium-sized saucepan or pot and cover completely with water by 2.5 cm/1 inch.

Bring to the boil over a high heat then reduce the temperature and simmer uncovered for about 50 minutes. Remove from the heat, drain and set aside. In a large bowl, make the dressing by whisking together the mayonnaise, yogurt, lemon juice, salt and pepper. Add the apples, pecans and wheatberries and using salad tongs or a large spoon, gently fold all of the ingredients together.

Plate the salad leaves first, then add the wheatberry mix on top. Serve immediately as the apple will discolour.

200 g/1 cup wheatberries

1 green apple, chopped

65 g/½ cup pecans

100 g/2 cups mixed salad leaves

For the dressing

50g/scant ¼ cup mayonnaise

50g/scant ¼ cup low-fat plain yogurt

3 tablespoons freshly squeezed lemon juice

½ teaspoon sea salt

½ teaspoon freshly ground black pepper

Serves 2–4

raw parsnip salad
with curry dressing

The poor parsnip has being playing second fiddle to the carrot for far too long. It's time to redress the balance. Slice it finely, avoiding the wooden core, and it can hold its own in any salad.

1 white onion, thinly sliced

150 ml/⅔ cup vegetable oil, plus extra for frying

1½ tablespoons curry powder

1 egg yolk

1 tablespoon mango chutney

1 teaspoon Dijon mustard

1 teaspoon white wine vinegar

freshly squeezed juice of ½ lemon

a small bunch of fresh coriander/cilantro, finely chopped

2 tablespoons warm water

4 parsnips, peeled

30 g/¼ cup cashew nuts

20 g/2 tablespoons raisins

1 sprig fresh mint, chopped

sea salt and freshly ground black pepper

Serves 4–6

Make the dressing. Fry the onion with a little vegetable oil in a frying pan/skillet until it begins to caramelize. Add the curry powder and cook for a further 2 minutes. Remove and allow to cool a little.

Put the onions in the bowl of a food processor. Add a little extra oil to the pan, scrape up the curry powder residue and add to the onions. Add the egg yolk, mango chutney, Dijon mustard and white wine vinegar. Blend to a paste. While blending, add the vegetable oil in a slow, steady stream so it emulsifies to a thick mixture. Add the lemon juice, coriander/cilantro and warm water to loosen. If it's too thick, add a little more water. Season to taste.

Using a vegetable peeler, peel the parsnips into ribbons. Discard the wooden core. Mix the parsnips with the cashews and raisins and dress liberally. Scatter with some fresh coriander/cilantro and mint leaves, and serve.

pearl barley, roast pumpkin & green bean salad

Pearl barley is great in salads, as it manages to retain a bit of texture and is one of the rare white ingredients, which makes it very useful for improving your salad aesthetics.

Preheat the oven to 200°C (400°F) Gas 6. Toss the pumpkin with a little olive oil and sea salt in a roasting pan. Roast for 20–25 minutes, until soft but not disintegrating.

In the meantime, bring a pan of salted water to the boil and cook the pearl barley for 20–30 minutes. It's impossible to give a precise cooking time, as each batch seems to be different (the same seems to apply to dried chickpeas, for some reason). You want the grains to be al dente, but not chalky or overly chewy. When they're ready, drain them and set aside.

For the beans, bring another pan of salted water to the boil and prepare a bowl of iced water. Add the beans and cook for 3–5 minutes. Test them by giving them a bend; you want them to be flexible but still have a nice snap if you push them too far. Once cooked, drain them and drop them immediately into the iced water. This 'refreshing' process will halt the cooking process and help keep the beans perfectly cooked and vibrantly green.

To assemble the salad, mix the pearl barley with the sundried tomatoes, olives, capers, red onion, basil and garlic. Add this to the roast pumpkin and green beans and stir gently until well combined. Drizzle with a little olive oil and serve.

500 g/1 lb. 2 oz. pumpkin, peeled and cut into 3-cm/1¼-in cubes

200 g/generous 1 cup pearl barley

olive oil, for roasting

400 g/14 oz. green beans, topped but not tailed

100 g/3½ oz. sundried tomatoes, roughly chopped

20 stoned/pitted black olives

1 tablespoon capers

1 red onion, sliced

1 bunch fresh basil, roughly chopped

1 garlic clove, crushed

sea salt and freshly ground black pepper

Serves 4–6

Choose from a range of classic dishes, such as Black Bean & Cheese Burrito and a comforting Vegetable Tagine to the more unusual but equally delicious Quinoa Burgers with Portobello Mushrooms and Millet-stuffed Squash with Caramelized Onions, Kale & Raisins.

mains

spinach & cheese burek

Burek is a baked or fried pastry, often surrounding a cheese and vegetable filling. Traditionally, in parts of Eastern Europe, burek is enjoyed with a glass of kefir, a type of drinking yogurt.

300 g/10 oz. fresh spinach
(or 420 g/ 14 oz. frozen spinach, defrosted and drained)

110 g/½ cup cottage cheese

100 g/scant ½ cup Greek yogurt

1 large (UK)/extra large (US) egg, beaten

30 ml/2 tablespoons olive oil, plus extra to brush

30 ml/2 tablespoons sparkling water

½ teaspoon bicarbonate of/baking soda

1 teaspoon salt

250 g/8 oz. large filo/phyllo sheets

18-cm/7-in. square baking pan (4 cm/1¾ in. deep), greased

Makes 4–6 portions

Preheat the oven to 180°C (350°F) Gas 4.

Blanch the spinach in a saucepan of boiling water for 30 seconds. Drain and squeeze to get rid of excess water. Chop finely, then put in a mixing bowl with the cottage cheese, yogurt, egg, oil, water, bicarbonate of/baking soda and salt and mix well.

Lay a filo/phyllo sheet in the base of the baking pan, leaving the excess pastry hanging over one side of the pan. Brush with oil. Lay another sheet on top so that the overhang is on the opposite side of the pan.

Spread a generous tablespoon of spinach mixture over the filo/phyllo sheet. Lay another 2 sheets over the filling and scrunch up the excess pastry to fit the pan. Brush with oil. Spread another generous tablespoon of spinach mixture over the filo/phyllo sheet. Lay another 2 sheets over the filling and scrunch up the excess pastry to fit the pan. Brush with oil. Keep going until all the spinach mixture is used up. You should end with a layer of filling.

Finally, fold over the overhanging pastry to cover the top of the burek and brush all over with more oil. If the top isn't entirely covered with pastry, add another sheet and brush with oil.

Bake in the preheated oven for 40 minutes until deep golden and risen. Remove from the oven and leave to cool for a few minutes. It freezes well – defrost and warm up in the oven before serving.

ricotta & spinach dumplings with cherry tomato sauce

Inspired by Italian cuisine, this recipe uses ricotta, together with spinach, to make little dumplings. The sauce here is a simple tomato one, flavoured with basil, lemon and a touch of chilli/chile for a hint of piquancy.

400 g/14 oz. fresh spinach

250 g/1 cup ricotta

2 eggs

100 g/¾ cup fine semolina, plus extra for coating

50 g/⅔ cup grated Parmesan (or vegetarian alternative – see page 4), plus extra for serving

salt and freshly ground black pepper

freshly grated nutmeg

butter, for greasing

For the cherry tomato sauce

2 tablespoons olive oil

2 garlic cloves, chopped

a splash of dry white wine (optional)

2 x 400-g/14-oz. cans of peeled cherry tomatoes

2 pinches of dried chilli/hot red pepper flakes or 1 peperoncino, crumbled

a generous handful of fresh basil leaves

a sprinkle of freshly grated lemon zest

Serves 4

Rinse the spinach well, discarding any discoloured or wilted leaves. Place it in a large, heavy-based saucepan and cook, covered, over a medium heat until the spinach has just wilted, so that it retains some texture. Strain in a colander, pressing out any excess moisture and set it aside to cool. Once cooled, chop the spinach finely, again squeezing out any excess moisture.

While the spinach is cooling, place the ricotta in a clean tea/dish towel in a sieve/strainer over a bowl to drain off any excess moisture.

For the cherry tomato sauce, heat the olive oil in a heavy-based frying pan/skillet. Add the garlic and fry, stirring, until golden brown. Add the white wine and cook, stirring, until it has largely evaporated. Add the cherry tomatoes, chilli/hot red pepper flakes and lemon zest. Roughly tear the basil (reserving a few leaves) and mix in. Season with salt and pepper. Cook, uncovered, for 5–10 minutes, stirring now and then until the sauce has thickened.

Place the ricotta in a large bowl and break it up with a fork. Mix in the finely chopped spinach thoroughly. Add the eggs, semolina and Parmesan (or vegetarian alternative) and mix well. Season with salt, pepper and nutmeg and mix again.

Sprinkle semolina on a large plate. Take a teaspoon of the ricotta mixture and shape it into a little nugget using a second teaspoon to help. Still using teaspoons, place this ricotta dumpling on the semolina and roll, lightly coating it. Repeat the process until all the ricotta has been shaped into dumplings.

Preheat the oven to 190°C (375°F) Gas 5, and while it's preheating, gently reheat the cherry tomato sauce. Generously butter a heatproof serving dish and place it in the oven to warm through. Line a plate with paper towels.

Bring a large saucepan of salted water to the boil. Cook the dumplings in batches, adding them to the boiling water a few at a time – you shouldn't over-crowd the pan. Cook over a medium heat until they float to the surface, around 2–3 minutes. Remove the dumplings using a shallow, slotted spoon, drain on the paper-lined plate, then carefully transfer to the serving dish in the oven to keep warm. Repeat the process until all the dumplings have been cooked.

Tear the remaining basil leaves and stir them into the cherry tomato sauce. Serve the dumplings with the sauce and a little bit of extra Parmesan on the side.

swiss chard, ricotta & pine nut tart

Ricotta gives this delicately flavoured tart an appealing lightness. Serve it with little gem lettuce leaves and a creamy dressing topped with chopped chives.

Preheat the oven to 200°C (400°F) Gas 6.

Firstly, dry-fry the pine nuts in a small frying pan/skillet over a medium heat. Shake the pan every 20 seconds to avoid burning them. Remove them when they're golden on both sides, then set them aside.

Next, make the pastry case. Roll out the pastry/pie dough on a lightly floured work surface. Use the pastry/pie dough to line the tart pan. Press it in firmly and prick the base to stop it from bubbling up as it bakes. Line the case with a piece of baking parchment and fill it with baking beans. Blind bake the pastry case for 15 minutes. Carefully remove the baking beans and parchment and bake for a further 5 minutes.

While the pastry case is baking, prepare the filling. Rinse the Swiss chard, then place it in a heavy-based saucepan, cover and cook over medium heat, stirring now and then, until wilted.

Drain it well using a colander, squeeze it dry and roughly chop.

Peel the shallots, halve lengthways and halve again crossways. Heat the olive oil in a separate small frying pan/skillet. Fry the shallots gently until softened, then mix in the balsamic vinegar and stir for 1–2 minutes until the shallots are glazed. Set aside to cool.

Lightly whisk together the beaten eggs, crème fraîche or sour cream and cheese. Season with salt and pepper and add the nutmeg.

In the blind-baked pastry case, layer in the glazed shallots, then top with the Swiss chard. Dot the ricotta, in small pieces on top of the Swiss chard and sprinkle over the pine nuts. Pour in the egg mixture.

Bake for 40 minutes in the preheated oven until golden-brown and puffed up. Serve warm from the oven or at room temperature.

50 g/½ cup pine nuts

300 g/10 oz. ready-made shortcrust pastry/pie dough

300 g/10 oz. Swiss chard

2 medium shallots

2 teaspoons olive oil

1 teaspoon balsamic vinegar

2 eggs, beaten

300 ml/1¼ cups crème fraîche or sour cream

50 g/⅔ cup grated Parmesan or vegetarian alternative (see page 4)

salt and freshly ground black pepper

freshly grated nutmeg

250 g/1 cup ricotta, drained in a sieve/strainer to remove excess moisture

23-cm/9-in. loose-based tart pan

baking beans

Serves 6

spaghetti with blue cheese, pecan & mascarpone sauce

The toasted pecan nuts add a lovely texture to this rich and creamy cheese sauce. A strongly flavoured blue cheese is perfect combined with the milder mascarpone.

4.5 litres/4¾ quarts water

450 g/1 lb. dried spaghetti

25 g/2 tablespoons unsalted butter

1 garlic clove, peeled and crushed

175 g/6 oz. vegetarian blue cheese, crumbled

175 g/¾ cup mascarpone

a pinch of ground mace or a little freshly grated nutmeg

salt and freshly ground black pepper

100 g/⅔ cup pecan nuts, toasted and roughly chopped

2 tablespoons chopped fresh chives

Serves 4

In a large saucepan over a high heat, bring the water to the boil and add 2 teaspoons of salt. Add the dried spaghetti, allow the water to return to the boil before turning the heat down to medium. Cook the spaghetti for 10 minutes if you like it al dente and a couple of minutes longer if you like it softer.

Meanwhile, melt the butter in a saucepan and gently fry the garlic over a low heat for 2–3 minutes, or until soft but not browned. Stir in the vegetarian blue cheese, mascarpone, mace or nutmeg along with the salt and pepper. Cook gently until the sauce is heated through but the cheese still has a little texture.

Remove the pan from the heat and stir in the pecan nuts and chives. Season to taste, then add the cooked spaghetti and mix thoroughly. Serve immediately.

wild mushroom & leek risotto

It's nice to think that a dish you associate with butter, cream and Parmesan can be just as enjoyable and indulgent when made with a few healthier alternatives. For example, substituting cream for soy cream/creamer gives this dish the same velvety smoothness. Soy cream/creamer has the same consistency as normal cream, and the slight difference in taste is undetectable in the risotto when seasoned properly.

Bring and keep the vegetable stock/broth in a saucepan just under boiling point, ready to add into the risotto.

Heat 3 tablespoons oil in a heavy-based pan, add the onion and leeks and cook gently over a low heat until they are completely soft and translucent. You do not want to colour them. Add 5 of the chopped garlic cloves, turn up the heat and stir for 1 minute. Add the rice, stirring frequently until the grains are completely covered in oil and beginning to turn translucent.

Pour in the glass of wine (it should steam and bubble) and season with a pinch of salt. Gradually add the hot stock a ladleful at a time, adding another ladle each time the liquid has been absorbed by the rice.

When the stock is finished, stir through the soy cream/creamer and some pepper. Season to taste, then turn down the heat.

In a separate pan, warm a little oil over medium–high heat. Add the mushrooms and fry for 1–2 minutes until the mushrooms have softened and coloured a little.

Add the mushrooms to the risotto. Make a quick parsley oil by combining the chopped parsley with the remaining chopped garlic clove and as much oil as you like. Drizzle over the risotto and serve immediately.

900 ml/3¾ cups vegetable stock/broth (make your own by covering carrots, onion, celery, bay leaf, parsley, thyme and a few peppercorns with water and simmering for ½ hour)

1 large onion, finely chopped

2 leeks, chopped

6 garlic cloves, finely chopped

350 g/1¾ cups Arborio or Carnaroli rice

glass of dry white wine

sea salt and freshly ground black pepper

200 ml/¾ cup soy cream/creamer

300 g/10 oz. mixed wild mushrooms

3 tablespoons finely chopped flat-leaf parsley

Serves 6-8

herby chickpea pancakes with halloumi and roasted corn & red pepper salsa

Serve these tasty pancakes as a light lunch or supper. The crunchy salsa can be made ahead of time and is also great added to salads.

Preheat the oven to 200°C (400°F) Gas 6.

To make the salsa, put the peppers in a roasting pan skin-side up, with the sweetcorn cobs and tomatoes. Sprinkle generously with salt and pepper and drizzle with 2 tablespoons olive oil. Roast in the top half of the preheated oven for 20–25 minutes until the skin of the peppers has shrivelled and the corn is golden. Reserve any juices left in the pan. Peel the skin off the peppers and remove the corn kernels from the cobs. Finely chop the peppers and break up the tomatoes with a fork, then put them in a bowl with the onion, chilli/chile and coriander/cilantro. In a separate bowl, combine the lime juice, vinegar, sugar and remaining olive oil. Season with salt and pepper and stir until well combined. Pour over the vegetable mixture and stir.

To make the chickpea pancakes, put the chickpea/gram flour, salt and cumin and turmeric in a bowl. Stir in the crushed chickpeas. In a separate bowl, combine the milk, egg, garlic and lemon juice and zest and beat well with a fork until well combined.

Make a well in the centre of the dry ingredients, pour in the milk mixture and stir from the centre until well combined. Add the chopped herbs, cover and set aside in the fridge for 20 minutes or until you are ready to cook the pancakes. Just before you make the pancakes, stir in the bicarbonate of soda/baking soda.

Lightly grease a frying pan/skillet and set over medium–high heat. Add a ladle of batter and cook until bubbles begin to form and the pancake starts to firm up. Turn it over and cook until both sides are golden brown and it has puffed up slightly. You can keep the pancakes warm in an oven (on a low temperature) until ready to serve.

Lightly oil the halloumi and cook over a high heat on a stovetop griddle/grill pan for 1 minute on each side until golden. Put the pancakes onto serving plates, top with the salsa and serve.

130 g/1 cup chickpea/gram flour

1 teaspoon salt

½ teaspoon ground cumin

¼ teaspoon turmeric

½ x 400-g/14-oz. can chickpeas, drained, rinsed and crushed

240 ml/1 cup milk

1 egg

1 garlic clove, crushed

grated zest and juice of 1 lemon

a handful of chopped fresh herbs

1 teaspoon bicarbonate of/baking soda

250 g/9 oz. halloumi, sliced

1 tablespoon olive oil

For the salsa

2 sweet red (bell) peppers, halved

2 sweetcorn cobs

a handful of cherry tomatoes

3 tablespoons olive oil

½ red onion, finely diced

½ fresh red chilli/chile, finely diced

a handful of fresh coriander/cilantro, finely chopped

freshly squeezed juice of ½ a lime

1 teaspoon white wine vinegar

1 teaspoon granulated sugar

Serves 6–8

potato waffles
with barbecue beans

Barbecue beans have to rank among the top comfort foods. Served here with delicious potato waffles, this recipe really is feel-good food heaven.

Preheat the oven to 200°C (400°F) Gas 6.

Prick the potatoes with a fork and bake them in the preheated oven on the prepared baking sheet for 1–1¼ hours (or in a microwave on full power for about 8 minutes per potato). Leave the potatoes to cool, then cut them open and remove the potato from the skins. Mash the flesh with a fork and discard the skins.

For the beans, heat the olive oil in a large saucepan or pot set over a medium heat. Add the sliced onion and cook until they turn translucent. Add the garlic to the pan and cook for a few minutes longer until the onion and garlic are lightly golden brown. Add the tomatoes to the pan and season well with salt and pepper. Add the Worcestershire sauce, soy sauce and dark brown sugar and simmer until the sauce becomes thick and syrupy. Put the beans in the sauce and simmer for a further 20 minutes. Keep the pan on the heat but turn it down to low to keep the beans warm until you are ready to serve.

In a large mixing bowl, whisk together the cooled mashed potato, flour, baking powder, salt, egg yolks, milk and melted butter until you have a smooth batter. In a separate bowl, whisk the egg white to stiff peaks. Gently fold the whisked egg whites into the batter mixture using a spatula.

Preheat the waffle iron and grease with a little butter.

Ladle some of the batter into the preheated waffle iron and cook for 3–5 minutes until golden brown. Keep the waffles warm while you cook the remaining batter.

Serve the waffles topped with the hot barbecue beans and grated cheese.

2 baking potatoes

260 g/2 cups self-raising/rising flour, sifted

1 teaspoon baking powder

a pinch of salt

3 eggs, separated

300 ml/1¼ cups milk

60 g/4 tablespoons butter, melted

a handful of grated Cheddar or Emmental, to serve

For the beans

1 tablespoon olive oil

1 medium onion, peeled and finely sliced

1–2 garlic cloves, peeled and finely sliced

400 g/2 cups canned chopped tomatoes

2 tablespoons Worcestershire sauce

2 tablespoons soy sauce

40 g/¼ cup dark brown sugar

480 g/3¾ cups cooked cannellini beans, drained and rinsed

sea salt and freshly ground black pepper, to taste

an electric or stove-top waffle iron

a baking sheet lined with baking parchment

Serves 4

squash & goat's cheese pancakes

Perfect for lunch, these pancakes are topped with sour cream or crème fraîche and drizzled with delicious pumpkin seed oil. Use a mild, creamy goat's cheese so that the flavour is not overpowering.

Preheat the oven to 180°C (350°F) Gas 4.

Put the diced butternut squash in the prepared roasting pan. Drizzle with the olive oil and sprinkle over the onion seeds, salt and curry leaves. Stir so that the squash is well coated in the oil and spices, then add the garlic cloves to the pan. Roast in the preheated oven for 35–45 minutes until the squash is soft and starts to caramelize at the edges. Leave to cool completely.

To make the pancake batter, put the flour, baking powder, egg and milk in a large mixing bowl and whisk together. Season with salt and pepper. Add the melted butter and whisk again. The batter should have a smooth, dropping consistency. Add about two-thirds of the butternut squash to the batter and set aside.

Remove the skins from the garlic cloves and mash to a paste using a fork. Whisk into the batter then crumble in the goat's cheese. Mix together gently. Cover and put in the refrigerator to rest for 30 minutes.

Put a little butter in a large frying pan/skillet set over a medium heat. Allow the butter to melt and coat the base of the pan, then ladle spoonfuls of the rested batter into the pan, leaving a little space between each.

Cook until the underside of each pancake is golden brown and a few bubbles start to appear on the top – this will take about 2–3 minutes.

Turn the pancake over using a spatula and cook on the other side until golden brown.

Serve the pancakes, topped with a spoonful of sour cream, a few sprigs of basil and the reserved butternut squash. Drizzle with pumpkin seed oil and sprinkle with freshly ground black pepper.

1 butternut squash (around 670 g/2½ lbs. in weight), peeled, deseeded and diced

2 tablespoons olive oil

1 teaspoon black onion seeds

a pinch of spiced sea salt or regular sea salt

4–5 curry leaves, crushed

1–2 garlic cloves, skins on

200 g/1⅔ cups self-raising/rising flour, sifted

2 teaspoons baking powder

1 egg

300 ml/1¼ cups milk

3 tablespoons melted butter, plus extra for greasing

125 g/1 cup soft goat's cheese

sour cream, to serve

a bunch of Greek basil (or regular basil if you can't find it) leaves, to garnish

pumpkin seed oil, to drizzle

sea salt and freshly ground black pepper, to taste

an ovenproof roasting pan, greased

a large frying pan/skillet or griddle

Serves 4

courgette & feta griddle cakes

These are quick and easy to prepare and make a great accompaniment to soups as an alternative to bread. The feta melts when cooked, giving them a lovely soft texture. These pancakes are made with raw courgette/zucchini, but if you prefer, you can fry them until soft in a little olive oil before adding to the pancake batter, making sure that you drain the courgette/zucchini of its cooking juices and cool first.

To make the pancake batter, put the flour, egg yolks, milk, melted butter and baking powder in a large mixing bowl and whisk together. Season well with salt and pepper and mix again until you have a smooth batter.

In a separate bowl, whisk the egg whites to stiff peaks. Gently fold the whisked egg whites into the batter mixture using a spatula. Cover and put in the refrigerator to rest for 30 minutes.

When you are ready to serve, remove the batter mixture from the refrigerator and stir gently. Add the grated courgette/zucchini to the batter with the feta and mint.

Put a little butter in a large frying pan/skillet set over a medium heat. Allow the butter to melt and coat the base of the pan, then ladle small amounts of the rested batter into the pan, leaving a little space between each. Cook until the underside of each pancake is golden brown and a few bubbles start to appear on the top – this will take about 2–3 minutes. Turn the pancake over using a spatula and cook on the other side until golden brown. It is important that they cook all the way through to ensure that the middle of your pancakes are not soggy. Serve immediately.

150 g/heaped 1 cup self-raising/rising flour, sifted

2 eggs, separated

250 ml/1 cup milk

70 g/4 tablespoons and 1 teaspoon butter, melted and cooled, plus extra for frying

1 teaspoon baking powder

1 large grated courgette/zucchini (around 200 g/7 oz. in weight)

200 g/1½ cups feta cheese, crumbled

1 tablespoon freshly chopped mint

sea salt and freshly ground black pepper, to taste

a large frying pan/skillet or griddle

Makes 10

2 medium–large beetroot/beets (around 500-g/18-oz. total weight)

2 teaspoons butter

2 red onions, finely chopped

2 garlic cloves, crushed

6–8-cm/2½–3-inch piece of fresh ginger, peeled and grated

400 g/2 cups plus 2½ tablespoons risotto rice, such as Arborio

200 ml/¾ cup plus 1 tablespoon white wine

850 ml/3½ cups vegetable stock

zest and freshly squeezed juice of 1–2 lemons, to taste

50 g/½ cup grated Parmesan or vegetarian alternative (see page 4)

3 sprigs thyme, leaves finely chopped

a handful of flat-leaf parsley, finely chopped, plus extra to serve

salt and freshly ground black pepper

Serves 4

beetroot risotto

A risotto is a great staple for everyday eating. This simple recipe is particularly tasty and its incredible colour will always be a conversation point too!

Preheat the oven to 200°C (400°F) Gas 6.

Individually wrap the beetroot/beets in kitchen foil and put them on a baking sheet. Bake in the preheated oven for about 40 minutes, or until tender. Set aside until cool enough to handle, then rub off the skin using the foil and cut the beetroot/beets into cubes. Set aside.

Melt the butter in a heavy-based saucepan, add the onions and cook over a low heat for about 10 minutes until soft but not coloured. Add 2 tablespoons of water to the pan if the onions are sticking. Stir in the garlic and ginger and cook for 1–2 minutes. Add the rice and cook until it turns opaque. Add the wine and stir until absorbed. Add a quarter of the stock and stir until all the liquid has been absorbed.

Continue to add the stock in stages, stirring constantly until the rice is soft but still has bite. Remove from the heat, then stir in the lemon zest and juice and the cheese. Next stir in the beetroot/beet and thyme, and season with salt and pepper. The consistency should be thick and creamy; add additional stock if required.

Spoon into warmed serving bowls and sprinkle with fresh, chopped parsley. Serve immediately.

chickpea & fresh spinach curry

Using a good-quality curry paste saves time, but for a fresh touch, this dish tastes great supplemented with fresh coriander/cilantro and fresh ginger. Chickpeas are popular in India and work brilliantly here in this spicy curry.

Put the onion, garlic and ginger in a food processor and process until finely chopped. Heat the oil in a frying pan/skillet set over a high heat. Add the onion mixture and cook for 4–5 minutes, stirring often, until golden. Add the curry paste and stir-fry for just 2 minutes, until aromatic.

Stir in the tomatoes, 250 ml/1 cup cold water and the chickpeas. Bring to the boil, then reduce the heat to a medium simmer and cook, uncovered, for 10 minutes. Stir in the spinach and cook just until it is wilted.

Stir in the coriander/cilantro and serve with the Indian bread of your choice.

1 white onion, roughly chopped

2 garlic cloves, sliced

1 teaspoon chopped fresh ginger

1 tablespoon light olive oil

2 tablespoons mild curry paste

400-g/14-oz. can chopped tomatoes

400-g/14-oz. can chickpeas, well drained and rinsed

500 g/18 oz. fresh spinach, stalks removed and leaves chopped

a handful of fresh coriander/cilantro leaves, chopped

naan or roti bread, to serve

Serves 4

vegetable tagine

This delicious Moroccan-style stew is a very versatile dish so you can use whichever vegetables you have to hand. Serve with plenty of couscous.

Preheat the oven to 180°C (350°F) Gas 4.

Heat the oil in a flameproof casserole dish set over a low–medium heat. Add the onion and cook for 5 minutes. Add the turmeric, cinnamon, paprika, ginger, chilli, garlic and orange zest and cook for 1 minute. Then add the peppers, sweet potato, aubergine/eggplant and carrots. Stir so that they are well covered with the spice mixture and cook for 2 minutes.

Stir in the apricots, tomatoes, honey and chickpeas. Then add the stock. Bring to the boil and cook on the stovetop for 2 minutes. Cover with a lid and transfer to the preheated oven to bake for 30–40 minutes. When the tagine is cooked, remove from the oven and stir in the spinach.

Spoon the tagine onto serving plates of couscous and top with the coriander/cilantro and yogurt, if desired.

2 tablespoons olive oil

2 red onions, quartered

1 teaspoon each ground turmeric and cinnamon

½ teaspoon paprika

1-cm/¾-inch piece of fresh ginger, peeled and finely chopped

1 red chilli/chile, finely chopped

2 garlic cloves, crushed

grated zest of 1 orange

1 red and 1 yellow (bell) pepper, roughly chopped

1 sweet potato, cubed

1 aubergine/eggplant, cut into chunks

2 carrots, sliced

50 g/⅓ cup dried apricots, quartered

400-g/14-oz. can chopped tomatoes

1 tablespoon clear honey or maple syrup

400-g/14-oz. can chickpeas, drained

500 ml/2 cups vegetable stock

a large handful of baby spinach

To serve

a handful of chopped coriander/cilantro stirred into Greek yogurt (optional)

prepared couscous

Serves 4–6

450 g/1 lb. dried haricot/navy beans, soaked overnight and drained

2–3 tablespoons ghee, smen or argan oil, or 1 tablespoon olive oil plus 1 tablespoon butter

2 onions, finely chopped

4 garlic cloves, finely chopped

2 red chillies/chiles, deseeded and finely chopped

2 teaspoons sugar

2 teaspoons harissa

2 x 400-g/14-oz. cans chopped tomatoes

a bunch of fresh mint leaves, finely chopped

a bunch of fresh flat-leaf parsley, finely chopped

a bunch of fresh coriander/cilantro, finely chopped

sea salt and freshly ground black pepper

1–2 lemons, cut into wedges, to serve

Serves 4–6

bean tagine with harissa & coriander

This is a classic Berber tagine, which can be found in infinite variations throughout Morocco using different beans – haricot/navy, borlotti, black-eyed, broad/fava or butter/lima beans. Often this dish is served on its own with chunks of bread, but it is also delicious served with thick, creamy yogurt and a Moroccan fruit chutney.

Put the beans in a saucepan with plenty of water and bring to the boil. Reduce the heat and simmer for about 30 minutes until the beans are tender. Drain thoroughly.

Heat the ghee, smen, argan oil or olive oil and butter mixture in the base of a tagine or in a heavy-based saucepan, add the onions, garlic, chillies/chiles and sugar and sauté for 2–3 minutes, until they begin to colour. Stir in the harissa and toss in the drained beans. Add the tomatoes and top up with a little water to make sure the beans are submerged. Bring the liquid to the boil, reduce the heat, put on the lid and cook gently for about 30 minutes.

Season the tagine with salt and pepper to taste, stir in most of the herbs and simmer for a further 10 minutes. Garnish with the remaining herbs and serve hot with the wedges of lemon to squeeze over the tagine.

2 tablespoons vegetable oil

1 large onion

2 teaspoons ground cumin

2 teaspoons dried oregano

3 garlic cloves, finely chopped

1–3 ancho chillies/chiles in adobo sauce, finely chopped

2 x 400-g/14-oz. cans black beans, drained

230-g/8-oz. can chopped tomatoes

250 ml/1 cup chicken or vegetable stock, or water

2 teaspoons fine sea salt

a pinch of sugar

200 g/1 cup cooked rice

4–6 large flour tortillas

180 g/scant 2 cups grated Cheddar or Monterey Jack cheese

sprigs of fresh coriander/cilantro, to serve

freshly ground black pepper

Serves 4–6

Adobo, bean & cheese burrito

These delicious breakfast burritos are a particularly great way to start the day, but they are fantastic eaten at any time.

Preheat the oven to 200°C (400°F) Gas 6.

Heat the oil in a large saucepan set over medium–high heat. Add the onion, cumin and oregano and cook for 5–8 minutes, stirring occasionally, until golden. Add the garlic and chillies/chiles and cook, stirring often, for 1 minute further.

Add the beans, tomatoes, stock or water, salt and sugar and mix well. Bring to the boil and simmer over a low heat for 10–15 minutes. Stir in the rice, then taste and adjust the seasoning.

Divide the bean mixture between the tortillas and sprinkle with grated cheese. Fold in the sides of each tortilla to cover the filling, then roll up to enclose. Place the filled tortillas seam-side down on a greased baking sheet or in a shallow dish. Cover with kitchen foil and bake in the preheated oven for 10–15 minutes just to warm through and melt the cheese. Serve hot, topped with sprigs of fresh coriander/cilantro and freshly ground black pepper.

ancho-roasted butternut squash tacos

This filling makes a nice change from some of the meatier ones usually found in tacos.

Preheat the oven to 220°C (425°F) Gas 7.

To prepare the squash, combine the onion slices, oil, cumin, oregano, chilli powder, salt and cinnamon in a large bowl. Add the squash and toss well to coat evenly.

Spread the spiced squash mixture on a baking sheet large enough to hold it in a single layer. Roast in the preheated oven for 25–35 minutes until well browned.

To serve, put a generous helping of squash in the middle of each tortilla. Top with a spoonful of sour cream and scatter over a few sprigs of fresh coriander/cilantro. Serve immediately with Guacamole, any hot sauce and lemon wedges on the side for squeezing.

1 large onion, halved and sliced

4 tablespoons vegetable oil

2 teaspoons ground cumin

2 teaspoons dried oregano

2 teaspoons ancho chilli powder

1 teaspoon fine sea salt

a good pinch of ground cinnamon

1.2 kg/2 lbs. 12 oz. butternut squash, peeled and cubed

8–12 corn or flour tortillas, warmed

To serve

sour cream

sprigs of fresh coriander/cilantro

guacamole

hot sauce (such as Tabasco)

lemon wedges

Serves 4–6

8 fennel bulbs

1 tablespoon olive oil, plus extra for drizzling

4 tablespoons white wine

100 g/⅔ cup wild rice

400 ml/1¾ cups vegetable stock

3 shallots, chopped

2 garlic cloves, crushed

grated zest and freshly squeezed juice of ½ a lemon

60 g/scant cup grated Parmesan or vegetarian alternative (see page 4)

a handful chopped fresh flat-leaf parsley, mint or chives

60 g/1 cup soft breadcrumbs (if using dried breadcrumbs, halve the quantity)

salt and freshly ground black pepper

For the fresh tomato sauce

4 vine tomatoes

1 garlic clove, crushed

2 tablespoons olive oil

1 tablespoon white wine

1 teaspoon sugar

1 teaspoon tomato purée/paste

a squeeze of fresh lemon juice

1 teaspoon balsamic or white wine vinegar

a handful of chopped fresh flat-leaf parsley, mint or chives

Serves 4

lemon & wild rice stuffed fennel with a fresh tomato sauce

This light and fragrant dish contains fresh herbs, fennel and lemon and is served with a light tomato sauce. It can be made ahead of time, then simply finished in the oven – perfect for dining al fresco in summer.

Preheat the oven to 180°C (350°F) Gas 4.

To prepare the fennel, cut a thin slice off the bottom of the fennel bulb so that it sits flat. Cut about 2 cm/¾ inch off the top of the fennel bulb, so that you can get to the centre of the bulb. Hollow the flesh out of the bulb's centre and finely chop the flesh. Set aside. Put a large sheet of kitchen foil on a baking sheet – enough to wrap the fennel, and put the fennel bulbs on top. Season with salt and pepper, drizzle with olive oil, pour in half the wine, then seal. Bake in the preheated oven for about 40 minutes, until the fennel is soft.

Put the wild rice in a saucepan with the vegetable stock and cook according to the package instructions. Meanwhile, heat 1 tablespoon of the olive oil in a frying pan/skillet. Add the shallots and cook over low heat for 5–10 minutes until softened but not coloured. When cooked, remove half the shallots and set aside. Add the reserved fennel, garlic, lemon zest and juice, the remaining wine and season with salt and pepper. Cover and simmer over a low heat until the fennel is soft, then turn up the heat until all the liquid has evaporated and the vegetables turn golden.

Add the cooked rice and half the cheese and season with salt and pepper. Finish with chopped fresh herbs. Fill the fennel bulbs with the rice mixture and top with the breadcrumbs, some chopped fresh herbs and remaining cheese.

To make the tomato sauce, blanch the tomatoes in boiling water for 10 seconds to remove the skins. Deseed, then finely chop the flesh and set aside. Put the garlic in a saucepan, add the reserved shallots and cook over low heat for 2 minutes. Add the olive oil and the wine. Add the tomato flesh and simmer for 5 minutes. Add the sugar, tomato purée/paste and lemon juice. Stir in the vinegar and herbs. Add a litte water to the sauce to thin, if needed. Serve the fennel warm with a spoonful of tomato sauce on the side.

gnocchi with rocket pesto

Classic potato gnocchi originate in northern Italy, where they are a staple food. They are served just with melted butter and Parmesan, or maybe a tomato sauce, but they are great with pesto made from peppery rocket/arugula and sweet, creamy walnuts. They must be made with a good floury potato to give them the correct lightness: they should never be like bullets, but puffy little pillows of potato.

To make the gnocchi, cook the unpeeled potatoes in boiling water for 20–30 minutes until very tender; drain well.

Meanwhile, to make the pesto, put the rocket/arugula, lemon zest, garlic, walnuts, olive oil, Parmesan, salt, and pepper in a food processor and blend until it is the texture you want. Scrape out into a jar, level the surface and pour in enough olive oil to cover.

Halve the potatoes and press through a potato ricer, or peel and press through a strainer/sieve into a bowl. While they are still warm, add 1 teaspoon salt, the butter, beaten egg, and half the flour. Mix lightly, then transfer to a floured board. Gradually knead in enough of the remaining flour to yield a smooth, soft, slightly sticky dough. Roll the dough into thick sausages, 2.5-cm/1 inch in diameter. Cut into 2.5-cm/1 inch lengths and shape into corks or pull each one down over the back of a fork to produce the traditional ridged outside and the concave inside. Put them on a lightly floured tea/dish towel.

Bring a large saucepan of salted water to a boil. Cook the gnocchi in batches. Drop them into the boiling water and cook for 2–3 minutes or until they float to the surface. As soon as they rise, remove immediately with a slotted spoon and keep hot while you cook the remainder. Toss with the pesto and serve immediately, topped with shaved Parmesan (or vegetarian alternative).

Note: The pesto can be stored in a jar, covered with a layer of oil, for up to 2 weeks in the refrigerator.

900 g/2 lbs. floury potatoes, unpeeled

1 teaspoon salt

50 g/4 tablespoons butter, melted

1 small egg, beaten

250 g/2 cups all-purpose/plain white flour

Parmesan, shaved, to serve

For the rocket pesto

100 g/3½ oz. arugula/rocket leaves

finely grated zest of 1 unwaxed lemon

2–3 garlic cloves

50 g/½ cup shelled walnuts

200 ml/¾ cup good olive oil, plus extra to cover

50 g/2 oz. Parmesan or vegetarian alternative (see page 4), finely grated

sea salt and freshly ground black pepper

Serves 4

For the tart shell

225 g/1¾ cups plain/all-purpose flour

a pinch of salt

130 g/1 stick plus
1 tablespoon cold butter, diced

1 egg yolk mixed with
2 tablespoons milk

For the basic quiche custard

180 g/generous ¾ cup double/heavy cream, or crème fraîche for a healthier option

3 large eggs

1 teaspoon Dijon mustard

30 g/scant ½ cup grated Parmesan or vegetarian alternative (see page 4) (optional)

salt and freshly ground black pepper

For the filling

1 butternut squash, peeled, deseeded and chopped

2 tablespoons olive oil

1 teaspoon fresh sage leaves, finely chopped

80 g/⅔ cup crumbled feta

a 23-cm/9-inch round tart pan

baking beans

Serves 4–6

butternut squash, feta & sage quiche

A basic quiche recipe is a useful thing to have in your cooking repertoire. There are many combinations of vegetables, cheeses and herbs that work well so this recipe can be adapted to suit your chosen ingredients.

Preheat the oven to 190°C (375°F) Gas 5.

Rub the butter into the flour using your fingertips until the mixture looks like breadcrumbs. Sprinkle the pastry with 1½ tablespoons of the egg and milk mixture, stirring it through with a knife. Use your hands to bring the dough together in the bowl but do not knead the dough. If the dough still feels dry, add another ½ tablespoon of the egg and milk mixture. Continue until you can bring the dough together into a smooth, firm dough.

Roll out on a lightly floured work surface, or between 2 sheets of baking parchment, until it is about 3-mm/⅛-inch thick. Use your rolling pin to pick up the dough and lay it over the tart pan. Gently push the dough down into the pan, making sure that the base and edges are well lined. Roll a rolling pin over the top of the tart pan to remove any excess dough and tidy the edges with your fingertips. Chill the tart shell in the fridge for 30 minutes until firm.

Lay a round of baking parchment slightly bigger than the tart pan over the tart shell, pushing the paper down onto the base. Fill with baking beans and bake in the top of the preheated oven for 15 minutes. After 15 minutes, remove the parchment and baking beans and put the tart shell back in the preheated oven for a further 5 minutes, until there are no grey patches and the surface of the pastry has a sandy feel.

To make the custard, put all the ingredients in a bowl and beat together until well mixed. Strain the mixture to form a smooth custard.

To make the filling, preheat the oven to 200°C (400°F) Gas 6. Lay the squash in a roasting pan and drizzle with olive oil, and add salt and pepper, to taste. Roast the squash for 30 minutes, until it turns soft and starts to brown. Allow to cool, then stir it through the custard mixture, along with the feta and sage. Spoon the filling into the tart shell. Bake in the middle of the oven for around 20 minutes, until the custard is just set but has a slight, even wobble towards the centre if you gently shake the pan. Serve at room temperature with a green salad.

carrot & leek tarte tatin

A savoury tarte tatin is a really simple way to make an impressive vegetarian centrepiece, perfect for entertaining. This recipe uses carrot and leek but would be equally good with sweet roasted tomatoes or shallots.

Preheat the oven to 200°C (400°F) Gas 6.

Put the oil and butter in a large frying pan/skillet with an ovenproof handle and set over a medium heat. Add the honey and cook until it bubbles and starts to turn golden brown. Add the garlic, ginger and balsamic vinegar, then lay the carrots in the pan. Roll the carrots around to coat them in the mixture, then top with the leek, using the leek strips to fill in any gaps. Add the white wine, cover with a lid and cook over a medium heat for 5 minutes. Uncover and cook for another minute over a high heat until the carrots are golden brown on the underside. Season generously with salt and pepper.

Cut the puff pastry roughly to the size of the pan and place it on top of the carrots and leeks, tucking the edges down the side of the pan. Put the pan in the preheated oven for 20 minutes until the puff pastry is well risen and golden brown.

Meanwhile, prepare the balsamic reduction. Put the balsamic vinegar in a saucepan set over a high heat and boil until it is has reduced by half. Turn down the heat. Add the brown sugar and honey and stir until dissolved. Bring the mixture to a simmer and cook until the mixture is glossy and syrupy.

When the tart is cooked, run a knife around the edge of the pan and turn the tart out, upside-down, onto a warm plate while it is still hot. Drizzle the tart with the balsamic reduction and serve.

1 tablespoon olive oil

25 g/2 tablespoons butter

1 tablespoon clear honey

1 garlic clove, crushed

1-cm/⅜-inch piece of fresh ginger, peeled and finely chopped

1 teaspoon balsamic vinegar

about 4–5 medium carrots or 12 small (around 400-g/14-oz. total weight), peeled but left whole

1 leek, cut lengthways into strips

2 tablespoon white wine

salt and freshly ground black pepper

375 g/13 oz. ready-rolled puff pastry dough, defrosted if frozen

For the balsamic reduction

150 ml/⅔ cup balsamic vinegar

50 g/¼ cup dark brown sugar

1 tablespoon clear honey

Serves 4

millet stuffed squash with caramelized onions, kale & raisins

Millet is a versatile and sadly underused grain. It is best eaten right after it is cooked as a substitute for couscous because it tends to dry out once it cools. Since millet is a hearty grain, it pairs well here with the soft sweet flesh of an acorn squash.

Preheat the oven to 180°C (350°F) Gas 4. Soak the raisins in water for 20 minutes then drain and set aside.

To prepare the squash, cut them in half and scoop out the seeds inside. You should have a decent size cavity that will eventually hold the millet stuffing. Put the halves on the prepared baking sheet. Drizzle with olive oil and salt and bake in the preheated oven, flat side down, for 40 minutes, or until the flesh is tender.

While the squash is cooking, toast the millet with the 2 tablespoons of butter in a large saucepan or pot over a medium heat for 3–5 minutes, until you can smell a toasty aroma. Add the vegetable stock and bring to the boil. Reduce the heat, cover and simmer for 20 minutes. Then fluff with a fork, turn the heat off and let it sit, covered, for another 5 minutes.

While the millet cooks, fry the onions, butter and olive oil in a large frying pan/skillet until translucent. Add the honey and cook until the onions caramelize. Then add the paprika, chilli powder and drained raisins. Stir for 3 minutes, then put the mixture in a bowl and set aside.

In the same pan, steam the kale by putting 240 ml/1 cup water in the pan. Add the kale and cover with a lid to steam for 8 minutes, stirring after 4 minutes, until the leaves wilt. Remove the kale with a slotted spoon and add it to the fried onion mixture.

Add the millet to the kale and fried onion mixture and stir so that the millet is coated in flavour. Adjust the seasoning with salt and pepper.

Once the acorn squash are baked, turn them over and generously scoop a large spoonful of the millet filling into each cavity. Serve hot.

80 g/½ cup raisins

2 acorn squash

2 tablespoons olive oil

a pinch of sea salt

95 g/½ cup dry millet

2 tablespoons butter

300 ml/1¼ cup vegetable stock (preferably low-sodium)

1 large onion, chopped

1 tablespoon butter

1 tablespoon olive oil

1 tablespoon clear honey

1 teaspoon paprika

½ teaspoon chilli powder

100 g/½ head of kale

sea salt and freshly ground black pepper, to taste

a baking sheet lined with aluminium foil

serves 2

3 tablespoons olive oil

1 onion, finely chopped

2 garlic cloves, crushed

75 g/½ cup black beans

120 g/1 cup cooked quinoa (see Note)

100 g/½ cup sweet potato, flesh scooped out

1 carrot, shredded

½ teaspoon ground cumin

½ teaspoon ground coriander

2 tablespoons fresh flat-leaf parsley, chopped

15 g/⅛ cup gluten-free breadcrumbs

5 portobello mushrooms

a pinch each of sea salt and freshly ground black pepper

To serve

1 avocado, sliced

1 large tomato, sliced

1 gherkin/pickle, chopped

½ red onion, sliced

a handful of fresh coriander/cilantro

1–2 tablespoons freshly squeezed lime juice

a baking sheet lined with baking parchment

Makes 5

quinoa burgers with portobello mushrooms

This is a great go-to veggie burger! Quinoa is moist and mixes with sweet potato and black beans to give it a meaty consistency.

Preheat the oven to 180°C (350°F) Gas 4.

Heat 1 tablespoon of the olive oil in a saucepan or pot over a medium heat. Fry the onions for about 3 minutes, until softened. Add the garlic and cook for another minute. Then add the beans, stir and cook for a few minutes longer. Remove from the heat and transfer to a large mixing bowl.

Lightly mash the beans with a fork until they're semi-crushed. Add the rest of the ingredients (except the mushrooms and remaining olive oil) to the bowl and mix well. If the mixture is too moist, add extra breadcrumbs. If it's too dry, add some more mashed beans.

Form patties with your hands and place on the prepared baking sheet. Bake in the preheated oven for 20–25 minutes, checking after about 15 minutes and turning once to ensure even browning. Once cooked remove from the main oven and keep warm in a cool oven or hot plate.

Increase the temperature of the oven to 200°C (400°F) Gas 6.

For the mushroom base, clean the mushrooms with a clean damp cloth/rag. Remove the stems and drizzle with the remaining 2 tablespoons olive oil. Season with salt and pepper and roast for 20 minutes.

When ready to serve, place each burger on top of a roasted mushroom and garnish with your choice of traditional burger toppings.

Note: To prepare a basic cooked quinoa, put 210 g/1 cup quinoa in a frying pan/skillet with 240 ml/1 cup stock and 200 ml/1 cup water. Bring to the boil then reduce the temperature. Cover and simmer for 20 minutes. Uncover, fluff with a fork and set aside for 5 minutes before using.

Round off your meal with one of a selection of fruity and creamy classic desserts, including a tantalizingly tasty Plum Frangipane Tart with Ginger Cream and the ever-so-simple Individual Hazelnut Meringues with Cream & Raspberries.

desserts

rhubarb, orange & vanilla fool with shortbread cookies

A fool is a traditional English dessert made of puréed fruit and whipped cream. It is very versatile and can be made with any fruit compôte. Here, cream is replaced with yogurt, which is healthier but just as delicious.

To make the shortbread cookies, preheat the oven to 180°C (350°F) Gas 4. Cream the butter, sugar and vanilla until light and fluffy. Sift in the flour, add the lemon zest, if using, and stir it through until the mixture forms a dough. Turn the dough onto a floured surface and roll out to a ½-cm/¼-inch thickness. Stamp out rounds, using a cookie cutter and put them on a baking sheet. Sprinkle each cookie with a little sugar and chill in the refrigerator for 30 minutes until firm. Bake in the preheated oven for 10–12 minutes, then transfer the individual cookies to a wire rack to cool. Be careful as you transfer the cookies, as they will still be soft but will firm up as they cool.

To make the fool, preheat the oven to 200°C (400°F) Gas 6. Arrange the rhubarb on a baking sheet and sprinkle with the caster/superfine sugar, orange zest and half the juice. Roast in the preheated oven for 15 minutes until tender, then transfer to a bowl.

Combine the granulated sugar in a saucepan with 4 tablespoons water, and set over a low heat until the sugar dissolves. Turn up the heat and boil for 2 minutes to make a syrup. Pour the syrup over the cooked rhubarb, add the remaining orange juice, and set aside to cool.

Put one-third of the rhubarb mixture in a food processor and blend to a purée. Set aside.

Beat together the yogurt, vanilla and icing/confectioners' sugar. Add the cooked rhubarb and stir to combine. Put a spoonful of the puréed rhubarb in the bottom of 4 glass serving dishes, then add the yogurt mixture, then swirl some more of the compôte through the yogurt. Top each bowl with a little crumbled shortbread and serve with a shortbread cookie on the side.

250 g/9 oz. rhubarb, washed and cut into pieces

2 tablespoons caster/superfine sugar

finely grated zest and freshly squeezed juice of 1 orange

2 tablespoons granulated sugar

500 g/2 heaped cups plain yogurt

1 teaspoon vanilla extract or vanilla paste

1 tablespoon icing/confectioners' sugar, sifted

For the shortbread cookies

110 g/½ cup unsalted butter

55 g/¼ cup plus ½ tablespoon raw brown sugar (e.g. Demerara), plus extra to sprinkle

1 teaspoon vanilla extract

180 g/1⅓ cups plain/all-purpose flour

grated zest of ½ a lemon (optional)

a 6-cm/2½-inch round, fluted biscuit/cookie cutter

Serves 4

plum frangipane tart with ginger cream

A frangipane tart works particularly well with apples, plums, cherries or apricots. If you don't have any fruit to hand, simply cover the base with a layer of jam and top with almond flakes.

300 g/10 oz. ready-made sweet shortcrust pastry/pie dough

For the frangipane filling

110 g/½ cup butter

110 g/½ cup plus
1 tablespoon sugar

2 eggs

1 teaspoon vanilla extract

30 g/4 tablespoons plain/
all-purpose flour

110 g/1 heaped cup ground almonds

400 g/14 oz. plums, washed, stoned/pitted and halved

For the ginger cream

150 ml/⅔ cup whipping or double/heavy cream

1 tablespoon icing/confectioners' sugar

2 tablespoons of syrup from a jar of stem/preserved ginger

1 tablespoon finely chopped stem/preserved ginger in syrup (from a jar)

a 23-cm/9-inch tart pan

Serves 6–8

Preheat the oven to 180°C (350°F) Gas 4. Roll out the pastry/pie dough on a lightly floured work surface. Use the pastry/pie dough to line the tart pan. Press it in firmly and prick the base to stop it from bubbling up as it bakes. Line the case with a piece of baking parchment and fill it with baking beans. Blind bake the pastry case for 15 minutes. Carefully remove the baking beans and parchment and bake for a further 5 minutes.

While the pastry case is baking, prepare the frangipane filling. Put the butter and sugar in a bowl, and cream together until light and fluffy. Add the eggs, 1 at a time, beating well between each addition and then add the vanilla. In another bowl, stir the flour and ground almonds together, then add them to the butter mixture and stir until they are well incorporated. Pour the frangipane mixture into the tart shell and evenly space the plum halves on top, pushing them down so that the edges are submerged. Bake in the still hot oven for 30–40 minutes or until the frangipane is golden, well risen and firm to the touch. Cool on a wire rack.

For the ginger cream, put the cream, icing/confectioners' sugar and syrup in a bowl and whisk until it forms soft peaks and the mixture holds its shape. Add the chopped stem ginger and stir it through the cream. Serves slices of warm plum frangipane tart with a spoonful of ginger cream on the side.

individual hazelnut meringues with cream & raspberries

For the meringues

3 egg whites

225 g/1 cup plus 2 tablespoons caster/superfine sugar

1 teaspoon vanilla extract

100 g/¾ cup hazelnuts (or pecans or walnuts), very finely chopped or blitzed in a food processor

16 Ritz crackers, crushed

½ teaspoon baking powder

For the filling

300 ml/1¼ cups whipping cream, well chilled

4 tablespoons/¼ cup icing/confectioners' sugar

50 g/about 2 oz. fresh raspberries, (mango and strawberries also work well)

2 baking sheets lined with parchment paper or 2 x 15-cm/6-inch cake pans, lined

a piping/pastry bag fitted with a large nozzle (optional)

Serves 6–8

This is a great go-to dessert recipe because it tastes fantastic and can be whipped up in no time at all.

If using baking sheets lined with parchment paper, use a pencil to draw an even number of 6-cm/2½-inch-diameter circles to show where the meringues will go (you will pipe or spoon the meringue onto these).

Preheat the oven 180°C (350°F) Gas 4.

Place the egg whites in a dry, grease-free bowl and, using an electric whisk/beater, beat the whites to stiff peaks. Gradually add the sugar to the egg whites, a spoonful at a time, bringing the mixture back to stiff peaks between each addition. Stir the vanilla extract through the meringue, then gently fold in the remaining ingredients.

Pipe or spoon individual meringues into the circles drawn on the baking parchment, or else spilt the mixture between the prepared cake pans. Bake on the middle shelf of the preheated oven for 25–30 minutes, until the surface of the meringue is crunchy but the centre remains soft and chewy. Transfer to a wire rack to cool completely before filling.

When ready to serve, make the filling. Whip the chilled cream and icing/confectioners' sugar together until just holding shape. Spoon some cream onto half of the meringues, add some raspberries and top with another meringue. Refrigerate until ready to serve.

caramel oranges with honey mascarpone & toasted pistachios

This simple dessert is low in fat, inexpensive to make and gives a light finish to a meal. It is especially good served after a Vegetable Tagine (see page 105).

150 g/¾ cup caster/granulated sugar

a handful of pistachios

2 sliced oranges, peel reserved and sliced into thin strips

freshly squeezed juice of ½ an orange

For the honey mascarpone

250 g/1 heaped cup mascarpone

1 tablespoon icing/confectioners' sugar

1 teaspoon vanilla extract

Serves 4

Toast the pistachios in a dry frying pan/skillet over a medium heat then put them in a clean tea/dish towel and bash with a rolling pin to break them up.

Arrange the orange slices on a serving dish.

Mix the orange juice with 200 ml/1 scant cup water in a jug/pitcher or measuring cup, and set aside.

Put the granulated sugar in a saucepan with 100 ml/1½ cups water. Set over a low heat and cook until the sugar dissolves.

Bring the mixture to the boil and cook until the mixture turns a dark terracotta colour. Do not stir the mixture while it is boiling, although you can gently swirl the pan occasionally. Carefully take the pan off the heat and pour in the orange juice mixture, 2 tablespoons of water and strips of orange peel. Be careful as the caramel will hiss. Stir the mixture to remove any lumps, and pour it over the orange slices. Leave it to marinate for an hour or so.

Beat the mascarpone with the icing/confectioners' sugar and vanilla extract in a bowl and serve with the oranges. Sprinkle over the toasted pistachios and serve.

orange, almond & amaretto drizzle cake

A light, moist and tasty flourless cake which is great for gluten-free eaters. As this is a whisked sponge/beaten-batter cake, the lightness and rise of the cake relies on incorporating as much air as possible. Carefully folding in the ingredients is essential so that you do not lose too much air.

200 g/2 cups ground almonds, plus extra to prepare the cake pan

1 x 240-g can apricot halves in fruit juice, drained (about 1 cup), with juice reserved

100 g/½ cup full-fat plain yogurt

6 egg yolks

180 g/1 cup minus 1½ tablespoons raw brown sugar (e.g. Demerara)

1 teaspoon gluten-free baking powder

6 egg whites

For the drizzling syrup

reserved juice from the canned apricots (about 4 tablespoons)

1 tablespoon honey or maple syrup

2 tablespoons raw brown sugar (e.g. Demerara)

grated zest of 1 orange

2 tablespoons Amaretto liqueur (optional)

a 23-cm/9-inch springform cake pan, greased and base-lined with parchment paper

Serves 6–8

Preheat the oven to 170°C (340°F) Gas 3–4. Dust the base of the prepared cake pan with ground almonds.

Whizz the apricot halves in a food processor until they form a smooth purée. Add the yogurt and whizz until combined.

Put the egg yolks and sugar in a bowl and whisk/beat the mixture until it turns pale and light and fluffy. Gently fold the apricot mixture into the whisked egg yolks. Combine the ground almonds and baking powder and fold this into the egg yolk mixture. Finally, using clean beaters, whisk/beat the egg whites to stiff peaks and carefully fold these into the batter until they are just incorporated and there are no big lumps of white. Scoop the batter into the pan and bake in the preheated oven for 50–60 minutes until a skewer inserted in the middle comes out clean. This cake tends to take on quite a lot of colour so you may wish to lay a piece of baking parchment over the top of the cake after 30 minutes if it is starting to brown too much. The cake will sink slightly as it cools.

To make the drizzling syrup, put the fruit juice, honey, sugar and orange zest in a saucepan set over a low heat, until the sugar has dissolved. Once the sugar has dissolved, bring to the boil and boil for 2–3 minutes to reduce the mixture until it is light and syrupy. Finally, add the Amaretto, if using, and taste.

Pierce holes all over the top of the cake with a skewer and spoon the warm syrup over the cake so that it is absorbed by the sponge. Serve the cake at room temperature, with an extra spoonful of syrup. This cake is sticky so it's best eaten with a fork.

peach pie with sunflower crust

It's easy to take seeds and blend them into a tasty crust; sunflower seeds, in particular, work well in a sweet crust. The secret to flavouring a summer peach pie is the almond extract, but be careful, as a little goes a long way.

Put the dry ingredients in a food processor and pulse to a fine crumb. Add the melted coconut oil and pulse again until the mix is combined. Remove from the food processor and bind together in your hands to form a pastry. Wrap tightly in clingfilm/plastic wrap and chill in the refrigerator for 30 minutes.

Preheat the oven to 180°C (350°F) Gas 4.

Once chilled, press the crust evenly along the bottom of the prepared pie dish and up the sides. Poke holes in the pastry case with a fork. Then place the pastry case in the oven and bake for 20 minutes or until brown in colour. Do not turn off the oven.

For the filling, bring a pot of water to the boil over a high heat. Make a cross at the base of each peach. Then drop them one by one into the boiling water for 30 seconds. Remove then put in an ice-water bath. This will allow you to easily peel off the skin of the peach. Once peeled, slice each peach into thin, even slices and place in a mixing bowl. Add the rest of the filling ingredients and mix.

Add the filling to the pre-cooked pastry case and set aside.

For the topping, mix all dry ingredients together in a large mixing bowl, then add the melted coconut oil. Mix together then, using your hands, crumble the topping all over the top of the pie, making sure you cover all of the peaches.

Bake the pie in the preheated oven for a further 35 minutes to cook the filling and topping. Leave to cool, then serve.

145 g/1 cup sunflower seeds

60 g/1½ cup quinoa flour

40 g/⅓ cup potato starch

60 g/⅓ cup sugar

¼ teaspoon sea salt

7 tablespoons melted coconut oil

For the filling

8–9 ripe yellow peaches

3 tablespoons coconut sugar

2 tablespoons almond flour

⅛ teaspoon nutmeg

¼ teaspoon almond extract

For the topping

30 g/¼ cup almond flour

40 g/⅓ cup gluten-free oats

40 g/⅓ cup quinoa flour

3 tablespoons coconut sugar

¼ teaspoon nutmeg

60 g/½ cup sliced almonds

5 tablespoons melted coconut oil

a 23-cm/9-in pie dish, greased

Serves 8

crunchy almond cheesecake

For the nutty crust

150 g/scant 2 cups flaked/slivered almonds

30 g/2 tablespoons butter, softened

For the filling

500 g/generous 2 cups cream cheese

500 g/generous 2 cups ricotta

4 large eggs

400 g/1¾ cups condensed milk

80 g/⅓ cup almond butter

1 teaspoon almond extract

For the topping

80 g/¾ stick butter

120 g/½ cup golden marzipan (or white marzipan if golden is not available)

100 g/scant 1 cup crushed amaretti biscuits/cookies

a 23-cm/9-inch round springform cake pan, greased and lined

Serves 12

The crunchy almond crust of this cheesecake is a perfect contrast to the creamy almond filling. If you wish you can serve some poached peaches to accompany it, or freshly whipped cream flavoured with amaretto.

In a dry frying pan/skillet set over a gentle heat, toast the flaked/slivered almonds until lightly golden brown, watching carefully as almonds can burn quickly. Tip into a bowl and set aside to cool completely.

Spread the softened butter around the sides and base of the prepared cake pan. Sprinkle the cooled toasted almonds into the pan and shake it so that the base and sides of the pan are covered with almonds. (Do not try to do this whilst the almonds are hot or they will melt the butter and not stick to the sides of the pan.)

Preheat the oven to 170°C (325°F) Gas 3.

In a large mixing bowl, whisk together the cream cheese and ricotta, then add the eggs, condensed milk, almond butter and almond extract and whisk until the mixture is smooth. Spoon the mixture into the almond-coated pan and bake in the preheated oven for 45 minutes.

Whilst the cheesecake is baking, prepare the topping. Melt the butter in a saucepan. Chop the marzipan into small pieces and mix with the crushed amaretti biscuits/cookies. Pour over the warm melted butter and mix together. For best results do this with your hands so that the biscuits/cookies and marzipan stick together in small clumps.

After 45 minutes' baking time, the cheesecake should be golden brown on top and still wobble slightly in the centre. Carefully sprinkle the marzipan crumbs over the top of the cheesecake (this is best done with the cheesecake still in the oven but only if you can do so safely without burning yourself). Bake for a further 15 minutes until the topping is crunchy and the marzipan has caramelized. Remove the cheesecake from the oven and slide a knife gently around the edge of the pan to loosen the cheesecake and prevent it from cracking. Leave to cool, then chill in the refrigerator for at least 3 hours or overnight before serving.

2 pinches of saffron strands

2 green cardamom pods

350 g/1½ cups cow's milk labneh (strained yogurt)

3 tablespoons icing/ confectioners' sugar, sifted

2 medium mangoes, peeled and sliced

1 tablespoon finely ground pistachio kernels

Serves 4

saffron & cardamom labneh with mango

This rich and fragrant dairy-based dessert is an exotic, pleasantly indulgent way in which to round off a meal.

Finely grind the saffron. Mix with 1 teaspoon of freshly boiled water and set aside to infuse for 15 minutes.

Crack the green cardamom pods and remove and finely grind the black seeds with a pestle and mortar, discarding the husks.

Fold together the labneh, icing/confectioners' sugar, cooled saffron water and ground cardamom, mixing in well. Cover with clingfilm/plastic wrap and chill.

To serve, divide the mangoes among 4 serving bowls. Top with saffron labneh, sprinkle with the ground pistachio kernels and serve.

Index

Note: Vegan recipes are denoted in bold